Devotional Programs

About

Bible Women

by

CLAUDINE WATTS DEVER

THE STANDARD PUBLISHING FOUNDATION
Cincinnati, Ohio

2803

1036857

TABLE OF CONTENTS

Chapter		Page
I	Sarah, Mother of Nations	5
II	Miriam, First Woman Singer	16
III	Deborah, a Leader in Israel	25
IV	Jephthah's Daughter, Woman of Mystery	34
V	Hannah, a Praying Mother	42
VI	Abigail, Woman Pacifist	51
VII	Mary, the Mother of Jesus	60
VIII	Martha, a Misunderstood Woman	70
IX	Salome, the Ambitious Mother	78
X	Dorcas, a Woman Full of Good Works	86
XI	Lydia, a Career Woman	95
XII	Priscilla, a Servant of the Church	104

HOW TO USE THESE PROGRAMS

The programs which follow have been prepared to provide one lesson each month for a year. Each program is built around a study of the life of a Biblical woman. Six studies are from the Old Testament and six are from the New Testament. These studies are as complete as the Scriptural record permits, and it is recommended that the person, or persons, giving the lessons read all the references given—those at the beginning of the programs and those scattered throughout the lesson.

The programs are so arranged that one person may lead in their presentation or several persons may take part. If it is desired, all persons present may have the opportunity to participate through a discussion of the questions that are provided.

The programs may be used by the women's council (in circles or in the general meeting), the missionary society, the ladies' aid, at ladies' class meetings, or as a series of devotional studies for mixed groups.

Hymns have been chosen to correlate with the theme of each lesson. All hymns suggested were chosen from the hymnal, *Great Songs of the Church*.

Chapter I

SARAH, MOTHER OF NATIONS

Scripture Background for Study: Genesis 11:27—23:20

Song Selections: 1. "Where He Leads I'll Follow"

2. "Faith of Our Fathers"

3. "Simply Trusting" (*prayer hymn*)

Prayer Period

Scripture Reading: Hebrews 11:1-16

The Bible Story

The love story of Abram and Sarai, for such it is, began in Ur of Chaldees, in an idolatrous age and in an idolatrous family. Both were descendants of Shem, son of Noah. Their immediate ancestry must have been familiar with the story of the flood, which God had sent to cleanse the earth of its widespread wickedness and pollutions, too grievous to be permitted any longer.

Noah was a righteous man, but his descendants quickly forgot the God of their father and soon were engrossed in the worship of idols. Although the knowledge of God seemed to be fading from the earth, the last rays of departing truth lingered still upon the tents of Terah. Abram, son of Terah, seems to have been blessed with clearer visions of Jehovah, the true and living God, for he was later chosen by God to become the head of a great nation through whom the knowledge of God would be kept alive, and through whom God's most precious promise to mankind was to be fulfilled.

Abram and Sarai were married, and continued to dwell in Ur of Chaldees until the voice of Jehovah called them to leave the land of their birth (Genesis 12:1-3). Though the plans of God were as yet clothed in mystery, this was no uncertain call, no product of the imagination. This was a voice positive and authoritative. An unknown and shadowy future was spotlighted by a distinct and definite promise: "in thee shall all families of the earth be blessed" (verse 3). The decaying

5

influence of idolatry was too strong, the moral soil too degenerate for this to be the proper setting for the fulfillment of the prophetic saying that the seed of woman shall "bruise" the serpent's head (Genesis 3:15).

Though the land of their nativity was dear to the hearts of Abram and Sarai, they obeyed the voice of God and started their journey to Canaan, accompanied by Terah and Lot, Abram's nephew. The first lap of their journey ended at Haran, where they remained until the death of Terah.

Abram was seventy-five years old at this time. Sarai was sixty-five and barren. How was the promise of God to be fulfilled? The signs of a visible inheritance were vague and the chances of an offspring were fading, yet they questioned not, they doubted not as they again took up their journey into the land of Canaan. The picturesque caravan of animals, servants, and family advanced along perilous trails into a treacherous and unknown country. Sarai herself was probably the most impressive figure in the whole array. Her name means "princess," and regal she was in bearing and character. In Abram's own words she was "a fair woman to look upon" (Genesis 12:11).

Fear and apprehension marked every step as they entered this strange land populated with fierce and barbarous people, whose eyes glanced suspiciously upon them and whose hands were anxious for plunder. Trusting their God who had started them upon this pilgrimage, they encamped on the plain of Morah near Bethel, where they erected an altar of worship to Jehovah. It was here that God reaffirmed His earlier promise to Abram.

As a grievous famine began to be felt, Abram determined to seek relief in Egypt. It is probable that he did this of his own volition and not by God's direction. In so doing, he brought grief upon his household. As yet, Abram's faith in God's promises had not wavered, but he possessed human weaknesses, and the Bible does not "cover" for him. He loved his wife dearly, and knew the power of her charms. As he approached Egypt, a corrupt and spiritually depraved country, his faith began to waver. Fearing for his own life, he condescended to a deceitful policy. He suggested to Sarai that she pose as his sister, which she readily agreed to do. She really was his half-sister (Genesis 20:12). Such marriages were a common custom in those days.

Abram's wavering faith brought him much grief, for when the Egyptians saw Sarai's great beauty, they took her to Pharaoh's court. He was so pleased with her that he showered many costly gifts upon Abram for her sake. At this point, God interrupted the natural course of events by sending plagues upon the house of Pharaoh, who seemed to understand that it was because of Sarai. He called Abram and rebuked him for not disclosing the fact that Sarai was his wife. Sarai was restored, unharmed, to Abram, and they went out of Egypt back toward the land of Canaan.

All this time Lot had evidently been traveling with them. Both Lot and Abram had become very rich in flocks and herds; besides, Abram had silver and gold and costly presents, which he had received in Egypt. It soon became obvious that the two kinsmen could not dwell together in harmony because of strife between their herdsmen. Abram magnanimously offered Lot his choice of the land. Lot chose the well-watered valley of the Jordan, and pitched his tent toward the wicked city of Sodom, leaving the dry and barren plains for his uncle. From Sodom, Lot was later taken captive by several kings, but Abram took 318 of his own trained servants and rescued him. Together, they returned to the plains of Sodom.

As the years sped swiftly by, Abram and Sarai waited patiently for the fulfillment of God's promises. We have no indication but that through all these trying experiences Sarai's love and devotion to her husband were above reproach, the bond between them growing stronger with each passing year, the intensity of their union increasing into a force so strong that nothing could destroy or diminish it. This may be surprising when we recall that Sarai was barren, which was a reproach to any woman. In those days, a woman became important in the eyes of her husband only after she had borne a son.

Eleven years had now passed since the promise of progeny

was first made to Abram. Not understanding the divine delay and blaming herself as the possible cause, Sarai became anxious, and with a willingness to forsake her own vanity, went to Abram and said, ''Behold now, the Lord hath restrained me from bearing: I pray thee, go in unto my maid; it may be that I may obtain children by her'' (Genesis 16:2). Abram obeyed the voice of Sarai, never questioning the righteousness of such actions. In that day polygamy was a common and accepted practice, though never divinely approved. According to ancient custom, the child born of such a union as Sarai proposed would be regarded as Sarai's own child. But Sarai's proposition was to bring her much grief and heartache in the years to come, for this child by the bondwoman Hagar was not the child of promise.

After conceiving a child by Abram, Hagar quickly forgot her mistress' generosity in exalting her from a place of servitude to a place of honor as concubine. She assumed airs, looking with disdain upon her mistress. Unable to endure this, Sarai reproachfully complained to Abram, ''I have given my maid into thy bosom; and when she saw that she had conceived, I was despised in her eyes: the Lord judge between me and thee'' (Genesis 16:5). As a result, Hagar, reprimanded by Sarai, fled into the wilderness, but God sent an angel to comfort her. She was bidden to return to the tent and become submissive to her mistress. Thus was born Ishmael, the son of Abram and Hagar, according to the flesh, but he was not the child of promise (Galatians 4:23).

Thirteen more years passed with no heavenly messengers repeating the blessed assurance from on high. History is silent regarding the events of those years, but we can well imagine the melancholy, the waiting, the silence, and the anxiety. Were they forsaken by the very God they had worshiped and followed through perilous journeys, through wars, famine, and family disputings? Those long, silent years may have been the inspiration for the words written by David many years later: ''Wait on the Lord, and keep his way, and he shall exalt thee to inherit the land'' (Psalm 37:34).

Finally, in Abram's ninety-ninth year God spoke again.

His former covenant was renewed, the seal of circumcision was given, and the names of the patriarch and his wife were changed to Abraham and Sarah. On this memorable occasion, God, for the first time, made it plain that the child of promise would be born of Sarah, saying, "I will bless her, and give thee a son also of her: yea, I will bless her, and she shall be a mother of nations; kings of people shall be of her" (Genesis 17:16).

The next incident in the story represents a beautiful picture of hospitality, which is the first such occasion mentioned in the Bible. Three travel-worn strangers appeared at Abraham's tent door one day. Desiring to offer his best, Abraham hastened to Sarah's tent and asked her to make cakes of the finest meal and bake them upon the hearth. He, himself, attended to the dressing of a tender young calf, which was cooked and served.

These men turned out to be angels sent from God to inform Abraham that Sarah would soon give birth to a son. According to oriental custom, Sarah remained in her own tent during the meal, but with true feminine curiosity she was listening to the conversation. When the announcement was made regarding the birth of a son, she laughed and said, "After I am waxed old shall I have pleasure, my lord being old also?" (Genesis 18:12). A later passage (Genesis 18:15) explains that she denied laughing because she was afraid. Her real reason for laughing is not clear. Could it be that her laughter came from a sorrowing heart and a downcast spirit rather than unbelief? (Proverbs 14:13.)

Not long after this, Abraham again attempted to pass Sarah off as his sister in the court of Abimelech, king of Gerar, but the results were the same as before. God intervened and Sarah was returned to her husband.

At last, the long-awaited promise became an actuality. Sarah gave birth to a son who was named Isaac. She experienced all the joys of a young mother, even to the nursing of the child at her own breast. God's wonderful power and unchanging love were manifested to her by life's most cherished experience, one she had long despaired realizing.

At the time of weaning when a great feast was in progress to celebrate the occasion, the old animosity between Sarah and Hagar blazed anew, culminating in Sarah's demand to her husband, ''Cast out this bondwoman and her son: for the son of this bondwoman shall not be heir with my son'' (Genesis 21:10). This was a grief to Abraham, but Sarah was upheld by the Lord in this demand. Hagar and her son were sent away into the wilderness where they met with hunger and thirst, but were finally rescued by the hand of God.

Sarah's cup of joy was now overflowing. The dreams of her youth and the hope of God's promise to her were realized in her son Isaac. Free from interference by Hagar and Ishmael, she went joyfully about her duties of motherhood. How proudly she watched over her child! Many were the hours she spent teaching and training him for the high place he was born to occupy; many were the prayers she offered in his behalf.

Though Sarah's trials had been many, the greatest of all yet awaited her. The Bible is silent regarding her reactions to Abraham's experience on Mount Moriah. We know it was a trial to her faith as well as his. We can only imagine her anguish of spirit as she watched her husband and son make ready and depart up the mountain upon which Isaac was to be sacrificed. She had no choice but to turn to the same omnipotent God who had miraculously given her a son in her old age. By experience, she knew that she could trust this God of love, mercy, and majesty. Anxiety and sorrow were alleviated, her faith justified, when she saw both her husband and son returning from the altar of sacrifice.

We have no record of Sarah from this time until her death at the age of 127. During all the years of her marriage, she enjoyed the love and companionship of a devoted husband. Her beauty had been the ornament of his tent, her loyalty and devotion the joy of his life. She had been the companion of his wanderings, the partner of his faith, and the sharer of his trials as well as his dreams. Isaac's life of piety and good will are a tribute to Sarah's motherhood. A short time after her death, he brought his own bride to his mother's tent, thus showing how deeply and fondly he cherished her memory.

Abraham buried his beloved wife in a cave in the field of Machpelah, which he had purchased for that purpose. His mourning for her was deep and sincere.

Character Analysis

1. *She was a distinguished woman.*

Sarah was a woman distinguished in many ways. She is the first woman distinctly portrayed in the Genesis story of the beginnings of man's history and development on the earth. Eleven chapters are at least partially occupied with the story of Sarah. She is mentioned once in Isaiah, twice in Romans, once in Hebrews, and once in 1 Peter. She is the mother in the Bible's first recorded miracle birth. She is the only woman whose age is given at death. Hers is the first burial recorded in the Scripture.

2. *She was a beautiful woman.*

Although Sarah was a beautiful woman, who on two different occasions was taken into the courts of kings because of her beauty, there is no indication that she was vain or proud or haughty, as is often true of beautiful women. We become so engrossed with the beauty of her character that we forget her fairness of face and body.

3. *Her husband honored her.*

It is much to Sarah's credit that her husband looked upon her as his equal. He never questioned her judgment in matters that were of equal importance to both of them. Although deeply entangled himself, he considered the settlement of the delicate situation of Hagar and her child to be entirely in Sarah's hands. "Behold, thy maid is in thy hand; do to her as it pleaseth thee" (Genesis 16:6).

4. *She was an obedient wife.*

Notwithstanding this freedom in the handling of family affairs, Sarah was an obedient wife. Her high concept of wifely duty constrained her to leave the comforts and joys of her native land to become a wanderer through strange lands, and to forsake the worship of idols for the worship of the true and living God. Her quick agreement to the half-truth that she was Abraham's sister was, undoubtedly, a manifestation of this characteristic.

5. She was a devoted mother.

God had said that He would make Sarah "a mother of nations" (Genesis 17:16), and her attributes of character bear out her worthiness of this title. Her great joy in motherhood is shown in her own words: "God hath made me to laugh, so that all that hear will laugh with me" (Genesis 21:6). Her concern and care for her child is shown by the manner in which she guarded him against the taunts of his jealous half-brother Ishmael. With dexterity she maneuvered both Ishmael and his mother into exile. It may be argued here that Sarah's spirit was not generous and the channel of her love too narrow and limited, but her defense is that her sole concern was for the welfare of her child. Was she not upheld in this by the Lord?

6. She had great faith.

Sarah's one outstanding virtue was, unquestionably, her faith in God and His promises. This virtue makes all her other good qualities stand out as beacon lights, underscoring them with power and beauty. This quality alone gives her a revered place in Hebrew history to the extent that she is honored in the "catalog of the faithful" in the Hebrew letter (Hebrews 11:11).

Her faith was sorely tried at times and she became impatient, yet the overall picture of her life shows her to be a woman of outstanding and abundant faith, which sustained her through the long years of her youth and middle age, even into old age. This hope in her old age is remarkable when we note that, according to Sarah's knowledge, no woman had even borne a child when the time of life had passed her by. Faith carried her through the hardships of constant travel, the adversity of famine, and the humiliation of living in the courts of strange kings preparatory for entrance into harem life. The spoken promise of God was truly precious to Sarah. She believed and trusted in God as she patiently waited.

In a Nutshell

1. The easiest way to become a "distinguished" woman is to obey the voice of God, for His ways are still the most unknown and the most unpracticed ways upon the earth today.
2. The beauty that endures is the beauty of the soul. A woman whose life is "hid with Christ" (Colossians 3:3) is the most beautiful woman in the world.
3. The happiest experiences of a woman's life are wrapped up in a well-regulated household, a contented husband, and disciplined children.
4. Sarah obeyed her husband, but since he was human and often wrong, the results were not always pleasant. The results of obeying God are always profoundly pleasant to His people.
5. Motherhood brings out the finest and most unselfish characteristics of a woman's nature.
6. Sarah's faith came by hearing the voice of God. Ours comes exactly the same way: "So then faith cometh by hearing, and hearing by the word of God" (Romans 10:17).
7. A half-truth is the same thing as a lie and "Lying lips are abomination to the Lord: but they that deal truly are his delight" (Proverbs 12:22).
8. It is extreme folly to do evil in the hope that good will come of it.

Discussion

1. Would the average woman of today rather be distinguished by her personal appearance, her personality, or her Christian graces?
2. What chance does a modern woman have to attain faith as great as Sarah's?
3. Do the consequences of our own evil deeds end with us?

Closing Prayer

Our Father, we thank Thee for the precious promises Thou hast given in Thy Word, beginning with the promise to

Abraham and continuing through the pages of the New Testament. We thank Thee that Jesus Christ came to fulfill the promise made so long ago, and that we, through Him, may eventually reach that land of promise He has gone to prepare for us. We thank Thee for the story of Sarah, and pray that our own faith may sustain us through life's many struggles, even as Sarah's faith sustained her through all of her many trials. We pray in the name of Jesus Christ, our Lord and Saviour. Amen.

The Leader's Notes

Chapter II

MIRIAM, FIRST WOMAN SINGER

SCRIPTURE BACKGROUND FOR STUDY: Exodus 2:1-10; 15:1-21; Numbers 12:1-15; 20:1; Micah 6:4

SONG SELECTIONS: 1. "Marching to Zion"
2. "He Leadeth Me"
3. "Have Thine Own Way" (*prayer hymn*)

PRAYER PERIOD

SCRIPTURE READING: Exodus 15:1-19

The Bible Story

Since biography is not the purpose of Biblical records, there are only brief sketches of many interesting people. This is true of Miriam, sister of Moses. Her life story is so closely interwoven with that of her illustrious brother and with the history of the nation that we must consider the highlights of that most interesting period of history.

After living in Egypt for several generations, the children of Israel had flourished to such an extent that Pharaoh, fearing a rebellion, put them under bondage. No matter how rigorous the state of bondage became, the Israelites still prospered and multiplied. In desperation, Pharaoh ordered all the male children to be slain at birth. During this trying time, Moses was born to Amram and Jochebed, who were of the tribe of Levi.

When Jochebed saw "that he was a goodly child, she hid him three months" (Exodus 2:2). We can only surmise how she managed this, for the other mothers all around her were seeing their sons cast into the river (Exodus 1:22). When she could no longer hide her baby, she made an ark of bulrushes, slime, and pitch, into which she placed him and hid him at the edge of the river. Perhaps she knew that the Egyptian princess came to this particular spot to bathe.

It is at this point that we first hear of Miriam. She was

a very young child at this time, probably only about seven years old. Her mother placed her nearby to watch over the baby, as he slept in the ark. The only way we have of determining that this child was Miriam is by considering Numbers 26:59 and 1 Chronicles 6:3 which give Miriam, Aaron, and Moses as the only children born to Amram and Jochebed.

We do not know how long Miriam kept watch over the child, whether only for a few hours or for several days, but we do know that she was faithful to her charge. When the princess and her maidens finally came, they discovered the ark, opened it, and found the baby crying. Whereupon, the princess said, "This is one of the Hebrews' children" (Exodus 2:6). Noting the tender concern of the royal princess for a child of the slave people, Miriam was encouraged to approach and ask, "Shall I go and call to thee a nurse of the Hebrew women, that she may nurse the child for thee?" (Exodus 2:7). Upon receiving the princess' instruction to do this, she hurried away and brought the baby's own mother, who was immediately hired to care for her own baby.

The scene closes here upon the story of Miriam, and we hear no more about her for about eighty years. Sacred history in no way associates her with Moses during the time he was considered to be the son of Pharaoh's daughter, nor during the period of his exile in the land of Midian. It was not until after Moses had received his high commission from God on Mount Horeb and returned to Egypt to work out the miraculous deliverance of his people that we again hear of Miriam.

We may be sure that she was not an indifferent spectator to all the momentous scenes enacted in the land of Egypt, scenes in which Moses and Aaron played a conspicuous part. The prophet Micah ascribed a prominent place of leadership to Miriam during this period: "For I brought thee up out of the land of Egypt, and redeemed thee out of the house of servants; and I sent before thee Moses, Aaron, and Miriam" (Micah 6:4).

Immediately after the Israelites had safely crossed the Red Sea into which Pharaoh's mighty army plunged to its death, Miriam had her greatest hour. She and Moses led the people in the singing of a song of praise to God for His deliverance of the people. It is not clear as to who actually composed the song. Since it is sometimes called the song of Moses and Miriam, we are led to believe that they composed it together. This song, also called the song of deliverance, is the oldest national anthem on record. It is a thrilling song of beauty and majesty, ascribing to God all the credit for delivering His people from the oppressor's hand.

Miriam's part in this glorious hour is well described in two verses of Scripture: "And Miriam the prophetess, the sister of Aaron, took a timbrel in her hand; and all the women went out after her with timbrels and with dances. And Miriam answered them, Sing ye to the Lord, for he hath triumphed gloriously; the horse and his rider hath he thrown into the sea" (Exodus 15:20, 21). Here we see Miriam as the most renowned woman of the nation. As she led in the song and dance of rejoicing, the women gladly followed.

Why she was called a prophetess is not clear. A prophet was one who came before the people to make known the will of God. A prophetess was the feminine counterpart. She said later regarding herself and Aaron, "Hath he not spoken also by us?" (Numbers 12:2).

We would prefer to leave Miriam right here, but as the story unfolds we must observe her fall, by an act of sedition, from an exalted place of leadership throughout the nation to a place of complete obscurity.

The record says that Miriam, along with her brother Aaron, spoke against Moses because of the Ethiopian woman he had married (Numbers 12:1). This sounds as though Moses had married a second time, and though the Bible does not tell us, it is probable that Zipporah, daughter of Jethro, had died. Miriam's resentment may have grown out of the fact that Moses had married a foreign woman. However, later events indicate that she would have felt the same if Moses had married a Hebrew. Miriam had been a leader for many years. Perhaps she had become "the first lady" after the death of Zipporah, and because of the prestige this gave her, she would have resented anyone who attempted to dethrone her. It was simply jealousy. She could not bear to lose the personal influence and prestige she had gained.

God heard the murmurings of Aaron and Miriam and reproved their sin. He called them, along with Moses, to the tabernacle over which the cloud of His presence was hovering. There He spoke to them in no uncertain terms as to whom He would use as a prophet to His people. He said, "My servant Moses . . . , who is faithful in all mine house. With him will I speak mouth to mouth, even apparently, and not in dark speeches; and the similitude of the Lord shall he behold: wherefore then were ye not afraid to speak against my servant Moses?" (Numbers 12: 7, 8).

When the Lord had finished speaking, the cloud removed from over the tabernacle, and Miriam stood before her brothers white with leprosy. Aaron, feeling a rush of compassion, perhaps a kindred feeling of guilt with her, appealed to Moses, "Alas, my lord, I beseech thee, lay not the sin upon us, wherein we have done foolishly" (Numbers 12: 11).

"Now the man Moses was very meek, above all the men which were upon the face of the earth" (Numbers 12: 3). Such a man would naturally be inclined toward sympathy and forgiveness. He was touched by this tender appeal from Aaron, and forgetting the rebellion of his sister, along with her ugly spirit of envy and pride, perhaps thinking of her only in the innocence and beauty of young girlhood when she watched so tenderly over his cradle in the Nile, he raised his loving heart in supplication to God on her behalf: "Heal her now, O God, I beseech thee" (Numbers 12: 13).

God heard the prayer of Moses and answered it, not according to the way he prayed, "Heal her *now*," but according to His own law regarding the handling of leperous persons (Leviticus 13). Favored daughter of the nation though she was, and sister of the illustrious Moses, she spent seven days outside the camp and was cleansed.

There is a peculiar analogy between Miriam's sin and her punishment. Just as the canker of envy was consuming her whole character and personality, so her punishment of leprosy would rot and decay her physical body. It is understood that her distorted mind was cured as well as her diseased body.

Nothing more is recorded of her until her death in Kadesh in the wilderness of Zin. We can only surmise that the remainder of her life was spent in seclusion, as is becoming to one who had been punished for sedition. Like her brothers, Aaron and Moses, she was not permitted to enter the Promised Land. Thus ended the colorful career of this interesting and truly great woman.

Miriam is the first woman mentioned in the Bible whose interest was national and patriotic in nature. She is the first woman singer mentioned, and it is to her credit that she sang to the glory of God and led the women of her nation to do likewise. In this, it seems that Miriam set a precedent, for in later years the women were wont to rejoice in song and dance when the armies were victorious in battle.

Miriam is also the first woman mentioned in the Bible who was a leader of any importance outside her own household. In spite of the serious mistake of her later years, we believe that Miriam retained an important place in the hearts of her countrymen. Her story has been preserved in part for us, and we cannot help but admire her courageous spirit and daring as her cry of exultation, ''Sing ye to the Lord,'' resounded throughout the camps of Israel. Though Miriam died and was buried without ever entering the Promised Land, her song will never die. The spirit of this, the first national anthem, lives on in the songs we sing, even until the present time.

Character Analysis

1. *She was courageous.*

Character traits show up very early in childhood. Many authorities claim that character is definitely molded by the age of seven. The argument about which is the greater character influence, inheritance or environment, may never be settled; but we do know that Miriam's strength of character did show up at an early age, and that she had a good mother whose influence was undeniably felt in the formative years

of her life. She was following her mother's instructions when
she stood guard over her baby brother as he slept in the
bulrushes by the river, but it took courage for a young child
to carry out such a difficult and dangerous task.

Many aspects of the lonely vigil must have struck terror
in the heart of the little girl. Was she afraid of the river
itself, or the crocodiles inhabiting the river? Was she afraid
of the approaching darkness, or the cruel Egyptians who
might pass at any moment? We do not know the answer to
these questions. We only know that, in spite of the actual
dangers and her own childish fears of imagined dangers, she
courageously kept her vigil.

2. *She willingly accepted responsibilities.*

Miriam's acceptance of the responsibility of keeping watch
over the baby Moses was an act far above what could nor-
mally be expected of a child so young. To watch over a baby
in the protection of the home is a simple task, and one which
has been delegated to young girls in every age from the dawn
of history until the present age. To watch over a baby under
the peculiar circumstances in this case was far from being a
simple task. Whether or not she felt adequate to deal with
any situation that might arise, she was willing to try, and
that often proves to be the most important thing, for one's
abilities cannot be tested or improved until he makes the
first effort.

3. *She was faithful to her duties.*

"If a task is once begun, never leave it until it's done" is
an old adage that may well apply to Miriam. She was not only
willing to accept an important task, but she also realized the
importance of sticking with it until it was finished. Faithful-
ness in discharging small duties is a preparation for larger
responsibilities. Jesus expressed it in these words: "Thou
hast been faithful over a few things, I will make thee ruler over
many things" (Matthew 25:21).

4. *She used her talents for the Lord.*

There were no schools in those days to develop talent, as

far as we know. Miriam's talent for singing, composing, and playing musical instruments were natural gifts from God, and she used them to glorify His name. The inspiration for her song was God's miraculous delivery from the Egyptians. The long years of slavery were over, and the people were free to serve their own God according to His directions and the dictates of their own hearts. They chose to begin their new era of freedom by first celebrating their victory over their enemies. Their very souls cried out in exultation and praise for their God, whom they fully trusted for the first time since Moses appeared on the scene with his God-given plan for deliverance.

The rhythm and melody of this song of Moses and Miriam have not been preserved for us, but we detect harmony in thought and spirit as Moses led the thousands of men in singing, "the horse and his rider hath he thrown into the sea" (Exodus 15:1), and Miriam led the women to answer with the same refrain, accompanied with dancing and playing of timbrels. What a time of rejoicing that was! And all in praise of God for His mercy and goodness.

5. *She was unselfish in her interests.*

The main interests of Miriam's life were national in spirit, her mission distinctly patriotic. She expended her energies in service to others. In childhood, her services were devoted to her baby brother; in adulthood, she served the whole nation. Her patriotic zeal forced her thoughts away from herself, and had she kept busy serving her nation, she might have avoided the tragedy that befell her in later years.

6. *She was submissive to God.*

Only one time is Miriam mentioned as a prophetess, yet that is proof enough of her submissiveness and response to God's instructions. God obviously cannot use one who is rebellious in spirit. The story of Balaam (Numbers 22) demonstrates this fact. The one time when Miriam deviated from this principle was the occasion of her sedition against Moses. Her proud spirit was humbled as she submitted, without a word, to the severe punishment given to her by God.

In a Nutshell

1. Courage is that quality of mind which enables one to meet danger and difficulty with firmness.

2. Baby-sitting is a profitable business today. Though **Miriam** was unaware of it, her "baby-sitting" was extremely profitable to the whole nation.

3. Sin is contagious. Miriam's sin led Aaron to sin, Aaron's sin led the nation to sin, etc. Righteousness is also contagious.

4. The heinousness of jealousy, like that of a hurricane, is found in its aftermath. Just as the hurricane marks its trail by wreckage and debris, so jealousy marks its trail by the disruption of harmony and the ruination of character.

5. Only the talents that are used are the ones that endure.

6. Leprosy can be looked upon as a type of sin. Just as Miriam had to meet God's requirements for the healing of leprosy, so we have to meet God's requirements for healing sin.

7. The journey of the Israelites through the wilderness to the Promised Land was a journey of faith and may be likened to our journey through this world to our promised land.

Discussion

1. Does the story of Miriam open a broader view of the possibilities for the use of our God-given talents?

2. Is this story an inspiration to women in exercising a healthier national spirit?

3. What is the best way to overcome the impulses to do evil?

Closing Prayer

We thank Thee, our Father, for the lessons we can learn from this study of the life of Miriam. We pray that we may broaden our own view of service to our country and our God. Help us to make better use of the abilities Thou hast so generously given to us. May we always be praising Thee in song and in deed. We ask in the name of Jesus. Amen.

The Leader's Notes

CHAPTER III

DEBORAH, A LEADER IN ISRAEL

SCRIPTURE BACKGROUND FOR STUDY: Judges 4, 5
SONG SELECTIONS: 1. "Count Your Blessings"
                     2. "Walking in Sunlight"
                     3. "All for Jesus" (*prayer hymn*)
PRAYER PERIOD
SCRIPTURE READING: Judges 5:1-13

The Bible Story

The entire record of the life and deeds of Deborah is short, being contained in only two chapters of the book of Judges. Practically nothing is told of her personal life, except that she was the wife of a very obscure man, Lapidoth by name, and that she lived under a palm tree between Ramah and Bethel in Mount Ephraim. In her song of victory over the Canaanites, she speaks of herself as "a mother in Israel." This is not necessarily proof that she was an actual mother of children, but may have meant that she "mothered" the people as they came to her for judgment.

The story of Deborah occurs in a very trying but interesting period of the history of the Israelite nation. After the death of Moses and Joshua, the people were left without a leader. The law of Moses, even though it was civil, moral, and religious in its import, was not sufficient to hold the people together in a common fellowship and purpose. Again and again, they strayed into the idolatrous worship of the heathen nations round about them. Because of this sin, God permitted the heathen kings to subdue them. When this foreign oppression became too grievous to be borne, the people would repent and cry to the Lord for deliverance. God always heard their cry and gave them help through a special leader who was valiant in battle, but whose victories came because he heard and obeyed the voice of God.

This period of history is generally known as the time of

the judges, and covers approximately three hundred years with fourteen different judges, one of whom was Deborah. The method of selecting the judges is vague, but at least one passage indicates that God did the choosing (Judges 2:16). In the case of Deborah, it is apparent that she became a judge of the people because of her sympathetic understanding of human nature and her wisdom in handing down decisions.

It must be remembered that these persons were more than judges, according to our understanding and use of the word today. Because of their natural superiority in wisdom and valor, they were accepted literally as rulers in every sense of the word. They were chieftains and heroes as well, and their leadership was especially sought in times of war. Considering this, it seems a little strange that a woman should be occupying the office of a judge. We can only surmise that the men of Israel had faltered in leadership, bringing about a general spirit of lethargy and defeatism throughout the land. Deborah's undaunted faith in God and her excellent patriotic fervor were the qualities most needed to arouse the people to action. Deborah was also a woman who had found favor with God, for the record says that she was a prophetess as well as a judge (Judges 4:4).

During the time Deborah sat under the palm tree of Ephraim judging Israel, the nation was at peace, but not very happy with the sad state of national affairs. For twenty years they had been oppressed by Jabin, king of Canaan. Such oppression in those days usually meant the destruction of vineyards, the exacting of tribute, the dishonoring of women, and perhaps the slaying of children. Many of the disillusioned Israelites were turning to the worship of idols. The people were afraid to rebel, for Jabin had nine hundred chariots of iron and perhaps a large army as well.

Being a righteous judge and having the welfare of her people at heart, Deborah could not countenance this demoralization of the nation. She contacted Barak, one of the nation's strongest military leaders, and told him that God had commanded him to lead the host of Israel in rebellion against Jabin. She let him know that she was not afraid of Sisera, captain of Jabin's army; neither was she afraid of his nine hundred chariots of iron. She convinced him that God and one are mightier than all the hosts of the wicked enemy. She probably reminded him of God's miraculous delivery of the Israelites from the mighty Pharaoh, through the Red Sea, to freedom in the land of Canaan. Was not this same Canaan given to them by the Lord as an inheritance and a dwelling place until the Deliverer should come?

Together Deborah and Barak devised a plan of action against the enemy. He was to select an army of ten thousand men from the tribes of Naphtali and Zebulun and go toward Mount Tabor close by the river Kishon. She assured him that God would deliver Sisera and all his multitude of chariots and men into the hand of Barak. Remember that Deborah was a prophetess, whose business it was to make known the will of God to man. Yet the fainthearted Barak said, "If thou wilt go with me, then I will go: but if thou wilt not go with me, then I will not go" (Judges 4: 8). This is a very strange and unusual statement for a military man to make to a woman, prophetess and judge of Israel though she was. Yet it demonstrates his confidence in her spiritual attributes and influence with the people.

Without hesitation, Deborah responded to Barak's wavering faith by declaring, "I will surely go with thee: notwithstanding the journey that thou takest shall not be for thine honour; for the Lord shall sell Sisera into the hand of a woman" (Judges 4: 9). Thus Barak was to be denied one of the honors of victory which would ordinarily have been his to claim.

Immediately, Deborah arose and went with Barak to Kedesh. According to plan, Barak selected his army of ten thousand men and continued to Mount Tabor, Deborah still accompanying them. It was here that she animated the whole army by this challenging prediction: "Up; for this is the day in which the Lord hath delivered Sisera into thine hand: is not the Lord gone out before thee?" (Judges 4: 14).

This prophecy shortly came to pass for all Jabin's chariots and all his army, down to the last man, were destroyed that

day. We do not have a full account of the battle, for the
record says only that the Lord "discomfited" them. It may
be that God used all the forces of nature against the enemy
in such a way as to give full advantage to Barak's army.
Deborah describes the scene in her song of triumph as follows:
"the earth trembled, and the heavens dropped, the clouds
also dropped water. The mountains melted from before the
Lord" (Judges 5 : 4, 5).

Sisera, the captain of Jabin's army and the only one remaining, fled to the house of Heber, the Kenite, who had
made an earlier peace with Jabin. Sisera sought refuge in
what he thought to be the household of a friend, but he had
not reckoned with Jael, the wife of Heber. While Sisera lay
asleep, she slew him by driving a nail through his temple.
Thus was fulfilled the prophecy of Deborah that he would fall
by the hand of a woman.

This is the end of the story of Deborah. Her glorious victory is best understood in terms of the last sentence of the
story: "And the land had rest forty years" (Judges 5 : 31).

Character Analysis

1. *She had a warm, sympathetic nature.*

It was perhaps this quality, which, first of all, placed her
in the position of judge and counselor of her people. Unless
one has a great feeling for humanity in general, and a special
interest in the underprivileged, it would be futile to undertake such an office. Her compassionate heart and loving spirit
were her two greatest assets as she listened to the personal
and social problems which the people came to discuss with her.

2. *She was unselfish.*

All this counseling with the people must have taken quite
a bit of time which Deborah, like most women, could have
used for her own selfish interests. But Deborah was not a selfish
woman, so she gave willingly of her time and talents in order
to bring happiness and contentment to her people. We have
no way of knowing whether she received any material com-
pensation for this service, but are led to believe that it was

not a paid service. If she received any remuneration, it probably was on the freewill offering basis, and was given only because the people loved her and were grateful for the help she gave them.

3. *She possessed great wisdom.*

While it requires a compassionate heart and a sympathetic understanding of human nature in order to be a counselor, it would be impossible to hand down fair and unbiased decisions when judging between two or more disputing parties unless one also were very wise. Where did Deborah get this wisdom? Could it be that she, like Solomon in later times, asked it of God? Many centuries later James was to write of this: "If any of you lack wisdom, let him ask of God, that giveth to all men liberally, and upbraideth not; and it shall be given him" (James 1:5).

While her great wisdom was invaluable in judging the people, it served a much greater purpose. It helped her to understand that her country was in great peril—perhaps in peril of complete annihilation by pagan tribes. She knew some action must be taken and taken quickly.

4. *She possessed patriotic zeal.*

Deborah's love for her country was intensified day by day as she talked with the people. When she realized how weak spiritually and politically they were becoming, her patriotic fervor came to the front. For a people who loved liberty and hated oppression, they had come to a very deplorable state indeed! The dearth of leadership among the men of her country only spurred her on until she became the living personification of the true spirit of Israel. Her burning patriotism was an inspiration to all who came into her presence.

5. *She possessed great faith.*

It must be said that all true leaders are men or women of great faith, and Deborah was not lacking in this virtue. Her patriotic zeal was useless without faith. All of the advantages were on the side of the enemy, but Deborah believed that God would be with His people. Never for one moment was she afraid of Sisera and his mighty chariots of iron. Her implicit faith in God and His promises was the force which prompted her to lead the nation into an aggressive war.

6. *She was a woman of action.*

Once it was understood that war was inevitable and the plans were made, Deborah did not hesitate to take action immediately. Many good causes have failed, fortunes have been lost, lives have been destroyed, and many well-laid plans have come to naught because people failed to take immediate action on what they knew to be right. This one characteristic alone was enough to make Deborah a great leader.

7. *She was humble.*

With all of Deborah's accomplishments and her victorious leadership in battle, there is no indication that she became proud or haughty. Rather we see a very humble spirit showing through the words of her song of triumph. She gives the first credit for victory in battle to God. She pays tribute to the different participating tribes for their bravery and compliments Jael for her part in the victory. In every line of the song, Deborah's meekness of spirit and her devotion to God is apparent.

8. *She was feminine.*

Throughout the whole story we never lose sight of Deborah as a woman. Never at any time do we get the idea that she gave up her womanly grace and took upon herself masculine characteristics in order to become a public figure. Had not the circumstances pushed her into political prominence, she would probably have been content to remain in the environs of her home, spending her energies for her own family and friends, as most ordinary women do.

Deborah was a leader and would be considered such in any age. All the above named characteristics did not make her a leader, for it is possible for one to possess all these and more, too, and still be totally lacking in leadership ability. A leader may be good or evil, but, in either case, he must be able to inspire others to follow. Just how is this done? We may be sure that a commanding personality and an indomitable will are necessary. Often circumstances are responsible. In Deborah's case, all these played a part. Who knows? Perhaps God raised her up and endowed her with the necessary attributes to carry her through to a glorious victory for His wayward people.

In a Nutshell

1. He who would be loved must first cultivate an unselfish nature.

2. Patriotism is not merely an emotion; it must find its expression in deeds.

3. Wisdom and understanding are like a husband and wife— together they constitute a team.

4. Faith undergirds all human endeavor.

5. Speech without action is like faith without works. They are both dead (James 2:26).

6. True humility is a rare virtue, yet who can be godly without it?

7. "If God be for us, who can be against us?" (Romans 8:31). God and one are always a majority.

8. Deborah was the political, military, and religious "first lady" of her country.

MY WORK

Find out what God would have you do,
    And do that little well;
For what is great and what is small,
    'Tis only He can tell!
                                    —*Author Unknown*

Discussion

1. Is the following statement true or false: "Leaders are born, not made"?

2. Why is a leader a leader?

3. Has our generation produced a woman of Deborah's caliber?

Closing Prayer

Our gracious Father in heaven, we thank Thee for the story of Deborah, and we are grateful that it has been preserved for us. We pray that this story will continue to be an inspiration to Christian women as they contemplate work in Thy church today. Give us all keener visions of things eternal, that we may have greater zeal in proclaiming Thy mighty works in the world today. Bless and sanctify a strong and loyal leadership in the church, so that tomorrow's world may be a better world. In the name of Jesus we pray. Amen.

The Leader's Notes

CHAPTER IV

JEPHTHAH'S DAUGHTER, WOMAN OF MYSTERY

SCRIPTURE BACKGROUND FOR STUDY: Judges 10, 11
SONG SELECTIONS: 1. "Trust and Obey"
                  2. "Sweet By and By"
                  3. "It Is Well With My Soul" (*prayer hymn*)

PRAYER PERIOD
SCRIPTURE READING: Judges 11: 30-40

The Bible Story

One of the most tantalizing stories of the Bible is found in the book of Judges. Scarcely had a century elapsed since the great victory of Deborah and Barak over the Canaanites, when, because of their open rebellion against God, the people were again plunged into oppression by the surrounding heathen tribes. It is here that Jephthah rises, like a star of destiny, to rescue prostrate and powerless Israel. The nameless daughter of Jephthah is linked in her tragic and beautiful history with that of her heroic father, whom the Scriptures say was "a mighty man of valour" (Judges 11:1).

Jephthah was the son of Gilead, a prominent man who lived in a territory by the same name. Since Jephthah was an illegitimate child, his brothers, under the pretext that he was unworthy to inherit along with them, banished him from his father's house and from his homeland. He fled to the land of Tob where, after gathering to him a band of "freebooters," he terrorized the countryside with his raids and conquests. While his activities were far from noble, his military prowess was genuine and his leadership unquestioned.

When the Israelites became involved in a hopeless war with the children of Ammon, they realized their need for a strong and valiant army leader. In desperation, the Gileadites, knowing Jephthah's reputation, sent a delegation of elders to

34

the land of Tob for the purpose of asking him to return and
become their captain of war. Remembering his earlier rejec-
tion from his homeland, Jephthah exacted a promise from
them that if he should subdue the Ammonites, then he was to
become the ruler of all Gilead. This solemn covenant was
ratified on both sides and Jephthah returned to the land of
his birth. Along with his daughter, an only child, he established residence at Mizpeh.

He first negotiated for a peaceful settlement with the
Ammonites, but this plan was rejected. Realizing that an open
encounter was inevitable and that his troops were ill-prepared
to meet the enemy, he sought to give them fresh courage, and
perhaps bolster his own confidence, by making a public vow to
the Lord. He declared, "If thou shalt without fail deliver
the children of Ammon into mine hands, then it shall be,
that whatsoever cometh forth of the doors of my house to
meet me, when I return in peace from the children of Ammon,
shall surely be the Lord's, and I will offer it up for a burnt
offering" (Judges 11: 30, 31). In that rash vow, Jephthah
exhibited a rudeness of character and a spiritual sightlessness
which was typical of the wild fighting man that he had been
in the land of Tob.

Jephthah's success in routing the Ammonites was phe-
nomenal. In a very short time, twenty of their cities had
fallen before his hand. Battle-scarred and weary, but elated
with his overwhelming victory, he hastened to Mizpeh where
he had left his daughter. As was customary at such a time,
the women and maidens had assembled to greet the conquer-
ing hero. The gaiety of the occasion was expressed in songs,
dances, and the playing of musical instruments.

As he drew near to his own doorway, who should come
out first to meet him but his own beloved daughter. Only then
did he realize how rash and cruel had been his vow. As he
looked upon his only child, the idol of his heart, standing in
front of his own tent door, all the glory of victory died out
of Jephthah. The scene was extremely touching. He stopped
dead in his tracks as she approached him in wild and joyous
dancing. The freshness of her youth, the radiance of her welcom-

ing smile, and the flash of joy in her eyes were but a reproach to him as he embraced her. From the depth of anguish and despair, he rent his clothes and cried out, "Alas, my daughter! thou hast brought me very low, and thou art one of them that trouble me: for I have opened my mouth unto the Lord, and I cannot go back" (Judges 11:35).

When she learned the nature of her father's vow, her heart did not falter even for a moment as she quickly responded, "My father, if thou hast opened thy mouth unto the Lord, do to me according to that which hath proceeded out of thy mouth; forasmuch as the Lord hath taken vengeance for thee of thine enemies, even of the children of Ammon" (Judges 11:36).

What an example of filial submission and spiritual fortitude was this! The only reprieve she asked was that she might have two months to go up into the mountains, along with some of the maidens of Israel who were her special friends, and bewail her virginity. This request was granted and, at the conclusion of the two months, she returned calmly and obediently to her father, "who did with her acccording to his vow which he had vowed: and she knew no man" (Judges 11:39).

Thus ends the tragic story of this heroic Hebrew maiden, except for a statement that it was a custom for the daughters of Israel to go yearly to lament the daughter of Jephthah (Judges 11:40). The marginal note says "to talk with." Still, a dark cloud of mystery hangs over her subsequent history. Did Jephthah really slay his daughter and offer her lifeless body as a burnt offering—a human sacrifice on the altar of religion? Or was there an alternative in carrying out his vow?

Bible scholars are disagreed upon this. Some commentators take this story literally, maintaining that she really was given as a burnt offering. Some contend that Jephthah intended from the first that a human sacrifice be made, but had little thought that it might be his own child. Other scholars point out a plausible alternative which can be justified by a careful study of the narrative.

They teach that the phrase, "and I will offer it up for a burnt offering" (Judges 11:31) can just as accurately be translated, "*or* I will offer it up for a burnt offering." This is suggested in the marginal notes of the Bible. Thus, if a human being were the first to come out the door, he would be permitted the choice of a life wholly dedicated to the service of God in the tabernacle, or a life given literally in human sacrifice. If an animal were the first out the door, there would be no such power of choice.

Let us take note here that it was a common practice among the heathen nations of that time to offer their sons and daughters as burnt offerings to their gods, but the Israelites were strictly forbidden to emulate such practices to their God (Deuteronomy 12:29-31). Furthermore, if any Israelite offered a human sacrifice to a heathen god, he was to be stoned to death (Leviticus 20:2). That the Israelites did at a later time "cause their sons and their daughters to pass through the fire unto Molech" is evidenced by the following references: Jeremiah 32:35; Ezekiel 23:37; and 2 Kings 16:3.

These phrases: "bewail my virginity" (Judges 11:37) and "she knew no man" (Judges 11:39) indicate that the actual fulfillment of Jephthah's vow could have been his daughter's pledge to celibacy for the remainder of her life. To a Hebrew maiden, this punishment was greater than death itself, for motherhood was her most cherished dream. Jephthah, too, suffered in this punishment, for it meant that his name and lineage died out of Israel.

While this intriguing story may leave many questions unanswered, there can be no doubt that the final chapter was tragic. Though our interest in the story may be wrapped up in its unsolved mystery, the real lesson for us is found in a character study of the girl herself. The story is not long, but it furnishes us with abundant material for study. Many centuries have passed and customs have changed, but the nobility of character embodied in this maiden of long ago still rates for her a place of recognition among the women of the Bible.

Character Analysis

1. *She was devout.*

Considering the upbringing of this girl, reared in exile amid heathen people in the wilderness of the desert, we marvel at her devotion to the God of her people. It seems doubtful that her father was much concerned about teaching her of the true and living God, for he was not noted for his devoutness. He was not recalled to his own country because of his spiritual attributes but because he was "a mighty man of valour." Yet somehow she knew the laws of God. Her total ambition was to conform strictly to those laws. Could it have been that she had a godly mother? She knew that once a person had committed himself to God in a vow, he was not to break or change it in any way (Numbers 30:2). This accounts for her willingness to comply with the terms of her father's vow, unfair and cruel though they were.

She loved God with her whole heart, so there was no hesitancy on her part about keeping the sacred vow, though the vow itself was not of her own making. We can imagine that her two months on the mountain, where she went to mourn her virginity, were spent in prayer and meditation. Thus her purity of heart and character sustained her during the days of preparation for complete obedience to the terms of her father's vow.

2. *She was meek in spirit.*

In her noble submission to her father's vow, Jephthah's daughter portrayed a meekness of spirit, which is amazing to us. The beauty and simplicity of such filial devotion is unbelievable to one living in the twentieth century! Yet this thing really happened!

Some may look upon meekness as a weak characteristic, but this is far from the truth. The meek of this world are undemanding by nature, unselfish in their interests, and unconcerned about their own personal comforts. The meek are willing to follow when following is right, yet ready to lead when it becomes necessary. Meekness is strength. In Zephaniah 2:3 we are told to "seek meekness."

3. *She was patient in suffering.*

Never a word of protest came from her lips when she learned of her fate. She did not bemean her father for his rashness in making such a vow. She never complained that the terms of the vow were unfair and too severe for her to meet. She did not ask for sympathy, yet this was given wholeheartedly and abundantly. Many of her friends, whose hearts were touched by her sad fate, accompanied her to the mountain of sorrow where they comforted her by their loving presence and daily ministrations. So great was the love of these friends that a yearly pilgrimage of four days' duration was made in remembrance of her.

Many centuries later, Jesus recommended some of these same virtues as a pattern for Christians to follow. It is a pattern that cannot help but bring happiness to all who hear and heed. "Blessed are they that mourn: for they shall be comforted" (Matthew 5:4). "Blessed are the meek: for they shall inherit the earth" (Matthew 5:5). "Blessed are the pure in heart: for they shall see God" (Matthew 5:8). Notice that these are accompanied by promises, which are extended to all who will heed the teaching.

In a Nutshell

1. Jephthah's daughter possessed godliness, meekness, and patience. Paul placed these virtues in the same category with righteousness, faith, and love (1 Timothy 6:11).

2. Meekness and weakness are not synonymous terms. Moses was meek "above all the men which were upon the face of the earth" (Numbers 12:3), yet who could call Moses a weakling?

3. Celibacy is neither conceived, condoned, nor condemned by God.

4. God provided for only one human sacrifice, and that was His only begotten Son who died on the cross to save us from our sins.

5. Paul says that a Christian is to present his body as a *living* sacrifice to God (Romans 12:1).

6. Why bargain with God (make a vow) when He has already offered us untold blessings through obedience to His Son?

7. God has a standing bargain which He offers to Christians: "Be thou faithful unto death, and I will give thee a crown of life" (Revelation 2:10).

8. When one has the love of God in his heart, it is easier to be patient in suffering.

9. When trouble comes, glory in it, for it sets up a chain reaction which leads to a brighter day: "tribulation worketh patience; and patience, experience; and experience, hope: and hope maketh not ashamed" (Romans 5:3-5).

Discussion

1. Do you believe that Jephthah offered his daughter as a human sacrifice?

2. Which is more important—to die for Christ, or to live for Him?

3. Is it possible to sacrifice for Christ?

Closing Prayer

We thank Thee, holy Father, for all the examples of heroic women in the Bible, and especially for this unnamed maiden of ancient Israel, who has left a heritage of courage and purity to all women. Help each of us to be more submissive to Thy will for us. May we learn, by Thy grace, to be patient in suffering, remembering how our Lord Jesus suffered and died for us. When indifference cools our ardor, revive Thy spirit within us and give us peace, for we pray in the name of Jesus. Amen.

The Leader's Notes

CHAPTER V

HANNAH, A PRAYING MOTHER

SCRIPTURE BACKGROUND FOR STUDY: 1 Samuel 1:1—2:26
SONG SELECTIONS: 1. "I Want to Be a Worker"
                   2. "Tell Me the Old, Old Story"
                   3. "I Gave My Life for Thee" (*prayer hymn*)
PRAYER PERIOD
SCRIPTURE READING: 1 Samuel 2:1-10 (*To be read between The Bible Story and Character Analysis*)

The Bible Story

Since the vast majority of the women of the world are mothers, the subject of motherhood is ever a timely and engaging topic. Motherhood is the most cherished dream of young girls, the richest experience of a woman's life. In searching the Bible for a woman who personifies the ideal in motherhood, we must choose Hannah, the mother of Samuel, for she stands alone in her spiritual concept of motherhood.

Hannah was the wife of an undistinguished priest named Elkanah, whose home was in Mount Ephraim. Hannah was not blessed with children, but Elkanah had another wife, Peninnah, who had several children, both sons and daughters. It seems probable that Hannah was the first wife and that she had been chosen for love and love alone. But since she had proved to be barren, Elkanah chose Peninnah as a second wife for the sake of progeny.

As was customary and according to law, Elkanah journeyed three times each year to worship God and offer sacrifices (Exodus 23:14). The law required that only the men appear before the Lord at the appointed place for the feasts and celebrations (Deuteronomy 16:16), but it was not forbidden that women and children go along. It was Elkanah's habit to have his whole household accompany him.

During these trips, Hannah's grief because of her barren-

42

ness was almost more than she could bear, for it seems that the jealous Peninnah chose such times to taunt and bemean her. On one occasion, Hannah was so disturbed over the situation that she wept and refused to eat of the feast, thereby causing her husband to demand, "Hannah, why weepest thou? and why eatest thou not? and why is thy heart grieved? am not I better to thee than ten sons?" (1 Samuel 1:8).

Hannah kept her silence, but when the meal was over she fled to the temple where in bitterness of soul and in tears she prayed, "O Lord of hosts, if thou wilt indeed look on the affliction of thine handmaid, and remember me, and not forget thine handmaid, but wilt give unto thine handmaid a man child, then I will give him unto the Lord all the days of his life, and there shall no razor come upon his head" (1 Samuel 1:11). The uncut hair was a part of the Nazarite vow of consecration to God (Numbers 6:1-5).

It seems that while Hannah lingered in prayer, she moved her lips but made no sound. She prayed silently in her heart. Eli, the priest, noticed this action and promptly accused her of drunkenness. Her answer proves her integrity and shows her serenity of spirit as she denied the unjust criticism. She answered Eli, "No, my lord, I am a woman of a sorrowful spirit: I have drunk neither wine nor strong drink, but have poured out my soul before the Lord" (1 Samuel 1:15). When Eli heard her story and learned of her eagerness for a child, he joined her in prayer, asking that God grant her petition.

Hannah left the temple in a joyful spirit, for she believed with all her heart that God had heard her prayer and would answer accordingly. She joined the family in worship before their departure the next day.

In due time Hannah gave birth to a son, whom she called Samuel, which means "asked of the Lord." After all the years of hoping, despairing, and praying for a child, her faith was justified. Her fondest dream had come true! Hannah was the mother of a son! What a beautiful picture she made as she hovered over his cradle, softly singing lullabies, tenderly ministering to his every need, and keeping watch while he slept. True mothers have always cared for their babies in

this manner, and Hannah was not lacking in the smallest
detail. She never left her child to the care of others. On
first occasion when her husband and the rest of the househ
made the journey to the tabernacle at Shiloh for their re
lar worship, Hannah declined to go because her baby had
yet been weaned.

Finally, soon after the child had been weaned, Han
took him to the temple along with a suitable offering,
there she left him "that he may appear before the Lord,
there abide for ever" (1 Samuel 1:22). While at the tem
she reminded Eli that she was the woman who had pra
for a son, and now that her petition had been granted,
had come to fulfill her vow. She said, "as long as he liveth
shall be lent to the Lord" (1 Samuel 1:28).

Hannah's sacrificial fulfillment of her vow was promp
by her love for God and she was rewarded accordingly,
God is gracious to those who love and serve Him. Eli bles
Elkanah and Hannah, and prayed, "The Lord give thee s
of this woman for the loan which is lent to the Lord"
Samuel 2:20). In later years, Hannah became the mother
three other sons and two daughters.

Nothing more is told of Hannah, except that each y
when she came to the temple, she brought a little coat wh
she had made for Samuel. Each tiny stitch was a symbol
love for her first-born son, given in answer to prayer. E
snip of the scissors represented a prayer for the contin
favor of God upon the child dedicated to His service.

What about the child? How did he progress? The rec
says, "the child Samuel grew on, and was in favour both w
the Lord, and also with men" (1 Samuel 2:26). This is ve
much like the statement made regarding the boy Jesus ma
centuries later: "Jesus increased in wisdom and stature, a
in favour with God and man" (Luke 2:52).

The long and useful life of Samuel, both as prophet a
judge of Israel during a very corrupt period, is a wort
tribute to a worthy mother. Samuel is one of the few Bi
characters whose stories are told in detail, about whom the
is nothing derogatory recorded. This is also a gracious tribu

to his mother—a mother who prayed for a son, then yielded
hi̇m in his tender years to the keeping of the Lord.

(The Scripture reading for this lesson is Hannah's tri-
umphant prayer, which she offered in the temple at the time
she took her young son Samuel to present him to the Lord.
This is a happy, fervent prayer of thanksgiving to a powerful
and loving God, who had brought a song to her lips and joy to
her heart. It is a revelation of the depth of Hannah's spiritual
nature.)

Character Analysis

She was serene by nature.

Hannah's serenity of spirit is obvious on many occasions.
When Peninnah goaded her because of her failure to produce
children, though she wept and refused to eat, she did not
retaliate or in any way cause a family dispute. When her
husband chided her, she still kept her silence. Her grief was
a personal matter and she preferred to keep it that way. When
Eli falsely accused her of drunkenness at the temple, she did
not display her feelings by an indignant outburst, as she
would have been justified in doing, but rather quietly proclaimed her innocence. Her dignified bearing and calm ex-
planation of her actions were all the defense she needed, for
Eli believed her.

She was humble before God.

Humility is a rare virtue, yet Hannah possessed it in great
abundance. In the first recorded prayer she offered at the
temple, she used the term "handmaid" three times in reference to herself (1 Samuel 1:11). This term means "servant"
and shows clearly Hannah's regard for her own humble estate.
The longer prayer of thanksgiving (1 Samuel 2:1-10) expresses her deep humility many times, but especially in the
sentence, "Talk no more so exceeding proudly; let not arro-
gancy come out of your mouth" (verse 3).

She was persistent in prayer.

Hannah believed God to be a prayer-hearing and a prayer-
answering God. She believed that God, and God alone, could

change her sorrowful state into a state of joy and fulfillment, so she prayed for a child. She prayed in faith and she prayed repeatedly. She prayed when her heart was burdened and she prayed when her cup of joy was overflowing. She prayed for herself and she prayed for others. She prayed for the poor, the barren, the wicked, and the saints. She prayed that the adversaries of the Lord might be destroyed. Can anyone claim greater persistence in prayer?

4. *Her actions were consistent with her prayers.*

Some people do not live according to the manner in which they pray. They may manifest humility in prayer, but arrogance in dealing with their fellow men. They may bargain with God at the altar of prayer, but quickly forget their part of the bargain just as soon as God has manifested His grace. Hannah did not make this mistake. She made a vow of consecration for her son long before he was born. When the child came, she did not forget her vow, but fulfilled it to the last detail. She did not forget to return to the temple and thank the Lord for His graciousness.

5. *She personifies the ideal in motherhood.*

Though the record of Hannah is short, it gives a picture of motherhood which is unsurpassed in beauty and unselfishness. No woman ever had a greater desire for a child, and no woman ever had greater devotion to her obligations as a mother. No woman ever displayed greater spiritual strength in giving up her child to the Lord. Through the ages, Hannah has been an inspiring example to all who have read her story.

Although Hannah is unsurpassed as a devoted and God-fearing mother, she does not stand alone as a mother who was willing to give her child to God. There are many modern-day Hannahs who spend years in training their children for lives of service to the Lord. Their wisdom, faith, and spiritual understanding make a beautiful picture upon which we gaze in wonder and admiration.

The following is an excerpt from a letter written by Mrs. E. G. Phipps to her son Charles and his wife, Mary Frances,

just a short time before they sailed to Italy in 1947 to become
pioneer missionaries in this distant Mediterranean country.
This beautifully worded but poignant letter, which lays bare
the innermost struggles of a mother's heart as she prepares
to part with her son, is proof of one such modern-day Hannah.
It is given here in the hopes that it will be an inspiration to
the many mothers who chance to read it or hear it.

My dearest Travelers for the Gospel:

You cannot know with what pardonable pride I ad-
dress you thus. If it were not for the consolation and
serenity of mind that comes with the thought of your
being not "just away" from physical proximity to us,
but really being ambassadors for Christ, I should be,
of all mothers, most miserable.

Right now you are starting on the preliminary stage
of a great mission. You are leaving us for a compara-
tively short time, that presages a far, far longer separa-
tion, that at present I dare not dwell upon in thought,
or I lose my courage.

The humanity of my motherhood cries out, "You may
never see them again after they leave the home shores.
Five or seven years can bring a lot of changes, and more
especially at your time of life. You can't be happy in
their leaving, when, just now, you are enjoying the
bloom of a tiny bud that you cuddled close to your fond
heart, nourished it, loved it, prayed about it, and anxi-
ously watched its growth—sometimes fearful, sometimes
confident, but always trusting God to protect that precious bud and bring it to a beautiful full bloom of Christian character."

Then, the spirituality of my motherhood has to take
a firm stand and say, "Oh, yes, you can be happy.
Your humanity just said you always trusted God to protect and bring that bud to full bloom. Are you going
to hinder that growth and God's purpose by being unhappy and unthankful for answered prayer? God has
blessed you and given you so much to be thankful for.
Send them out with a smile."

So emotions are mixed, and a struggle goes on,
with the spiritual thermometer vacillating at weak mo-
ments of self-thought. I wish I could be strong at all
times. It isn't easy to let you go. My resignation to the
plan and my satisfaction and pride in your development

are not indications that maternal love is lacking or waning. If that were true, there could be no wrench that hurts the heart. For your sakes, we must hide the weakness of our humanity and dwell only on our happiness that we are co-workers with you and God, if we do not withhold from Him what is rightfully His from the beginning. He just loaned you to us for a while, and we are grateful. Now, as we give you back to Him, we do trust Him to protect you still, whether near us or far from us.

In a Nutshell

1. Joint devotions of a family should put an end to divisions in it. But, on the other hand, if the devotions put not an end to divisions, then let not the divisions put an end to the devotions.

2. Spiritual serenity enhances a woman's personality, stabilizes her character, and beautifies her soul.

3. Humility is a great asset in bridging the gulf between God and man, while arrogance is a hindrance, often making the breach wider.

4. Hannah's thank-you prayer was much longer than her prayer of petition. God's blessings always overbalance our needs.

5. Hannah asked, she received, she gave. Jesus said, ''Every one that asketh receiveth'' (Matthew 7:8)—then what?

6. What a pity that a praying woman should be taken for a drunken woman, when the contrast is so great.

Discussion

1. Is it true that only God can convert a woman into a mother?

2. Is it possible for a woman to dedicate her unborn child to God?

3. In this modern day of medical and scientific knowledge, is it right for a woman to pray that God will give her a child?

Closing Prayer

Our loving Father in heaven, we thank Thee for the story of Hannah—for her beautiful consecration as a mother and her excellent example in prayer. Help us to understand that true motherhood begins in consecration to Thee and grows only as we grow in Christ. May we not forget that a dedicated child presupposes a dedicated mother. Wilt Thou direct all the mothers in our midst and throughout our land to become praying mothers, that their sons and daughters may rise up and call upon Thy name. In the name of Christ we pray. Amen.

The Leader's Notes

CHAPTER VI

ABIGAIL, WOMAN PACIFIST

SCRIPTURE BACKGROUND FOR STUDY: 1 Samuel 25:1-44; 27:3; 30:5; 2 Samuel 2:2; 3:3; 1 Chronicles 3:1

SONG SELECTIONS: 1. "Higher Ground"
                 2. "Love Divine"
                 3. "Saviour, Like a Shepherd Lead Us"
                    (*prayer hymn*)

PRAYER PERIOD

SCRIPTURE READING: Psalm 37:1-20

The Bible Story

The first book of Samuel relates a beautiful story about a beautiful woman. Few would recognize Abigail as one of the outstanding women of the Old Testament; many would call her obscure. Certainly her story is not long or momentous, but it is an excellent character portrayal. However, her story is not told because of the excellency of her character. It is told only because of her close association with David, and is incidental in the unfolding of the history of that period. The purpose of the Bible is not to extol character.

When David was a fugitive from Saul, roaming the desert and mountain country round about Canaan, he gathered to him a following of several hundred men. They acted as bodyguard and protector from Saul's army, but many times they engaged in minor skirmishes with the heathen tribes who were constantly raiding the outlying areas of Israel.

David and this band of warriors were often a wall of protection to the herdsmen in the valleys round about. One such man was Nabal, a man of Maon, near Carmel. He was a very rich man, possessing three thousand sheep and a thousand goats. Abigail was his wife. The record says, "she was a woman of good understanding, and of a beautiful countenance: but the man was churlish and evil in his doings" (1 Samuel 25:3).

51

When sheepshearing season came, Nabal made a great feast for his helpers. Many friends and neighbors gathered for the festivities. It can be imagined that a rich man like Nabal would provide generously for his guests at such a time. Being a good wife and a virtuous woman, Abigail would not neglect her duties as hostess for the occasion.

Not far away in the wilderness of Paran, David and his men were encamped. Provisions were growing short and the men were hungry. David heard that Nabal was shearing his sheep and knew that there would be an abundance of food available at his camp. He sent ten of his young men to Nabal at Carmel with a proper greeting and a request for some food. The request was polite and just, and David had every reason to expect it to be granted, but the answer from Nabal was curt and insulting. He said, "Who is David? and who is the son of Jesse? there be many servants now a days that break away every man from his master. Shall I then take my bread, and my water, and my flesh that I have killed for my shearers, and give it unto men, whom I know not whence they be?" (1 Samuel 25:10, 11).

When the young men returned to David with this message, he replied, "Surely in vain have I kept all that this fellow hath in the wilderness, so that nothing was missed of all that pertained unto him: and he hath requited me evil for good" (1 Samuel 25:21). Then he began immediate preparations for war against the house of Nabal. Four hundred of his men took up their swords and made ready to avenge this insult to David.

Meanwhile, another scene was taking place. One of Nabal's servants went to Abigail and told her of her husband's rash treatment of David's men. He reminded her of the injustice of this action by saying of David's men: "They were a wall unto us both by night and day, all the while we were with them keeping the sheep" (1 Samuel 25:16). This servant knew that the whole household was in grave danger at the hand of David, and he evidently had confidence in Abigail's understanding of the situation. This confidence was wholly justified as we shall see in the ensuing events.

Wise woman that she was, Abigail lost no time lamenting the threatened danger to her household. She knew what happened when strong-minded men like David were provoked to wrath, and she also knew the futility of a discussion with her drunken husband. Knowing that their only hope lay in quick action, she made haste to prepare a generous donation of provisions to send to David. She supervised the baking of two hundred loaves of bread and had five sheep dressed. Along with these she collected five measures of parched corn, one hundred clusters of raisins, two hundred cakes of figs, and two bottles of wine. The food was loaded upon asses and sent ahead of servants, but Abigail herself mounted another ass and followed until they met with David by the covert of the hill.

With this encounter, Abigail dismounted the ass, fell upon her face before David and made a beautiful, touching speech. She admitted to her husband's stupidity and apologized for his bad manners, explaining that she herself knew nothing of his treatment of David's young men. She begged David to forgive all trespasses against him and to receive the food she had brought. She praised him for his inherent goodness and brought to his remembrance the Lord's blessings to him in that he was to be the ruler of all Israel. In beautiful expression, she depicted David's future relationship with the Lord of Israel: "the soul of my lord shall be bound in the bundle of life with the Lord thy God" (1 Samuel 25:29). And, last of all, Abigail besought David not to shed blood needlessly or to avenge himself under cover of anger, for the time would come when such action would be grievous to him, in that the innocent would suffer along with the guilty.

So impressed was David with the earnest petition and sound advice of this courageous woman that his heart was touched as he replied, "Blessed be the Lord God of Israel, which sent thee this day to meet me: and blessed be thy advice" (1 Samuel 25:32, 33). Then he accepted her food and sent her home with his blessings.

When Nabal was sober enough to understand what she was talking about, Abigail told him all that had happened.

He was so frightened that he relapsed into a coma and died within ten days. David learned of the death of Nabal, and his heart went out to Abigail in affection. He remembered her quiet dignity and beautiful countenance as she conversed with him by the mountainside. He sent messengers to her, requesting that she become his wife.

Although she felt unworthy to be the wife of God's chosen ruler, she answered the messengers, "Behold, let thine handmaid be a servant to wash the feet of the servants of my lord" (1 Samuel 25:41). Thus in humility she married David. She brought to his camp a large retinue of servants and her entire estate, thus increasing his material wealth and social prominence in the community. But these gains were far less important than was her stabilizing influence upon the character of the impetuous David.

She lived with David in Gath and in Hebron where she gave birth to their son, Chileab. After this, we know very little of the life of Abigail. We do know that it was not an easy life, for she was constantly exposed to dangers from the desert, dangers from Saul, and dangers from the warring heathen nations. At one time she was taken captive by the Amalekites, but was later rescued by David.

Although David had several other wives, Abigail was the wisest of them all, and must have influenced his decisions to a very great extent. Her gentle ways and wise counsel helped him to learn patience and forbearance. The truth of the proverb which says of a virtuous woman: "The heart of her husband doth safely trust in her" (Proverbs 31:11), is exemplified in the story of Abigail and her husband David.

Character Analysis

1. *She was a woman of beautiful countenance.*

While we do not have a complete description of Abigail's person, the record does say that she was of a beautiful countenance. This may or may not have reference to her facial beauty. It may merely refer to the expression of her face, such as an open countenance or pleasing expression, which

comes from a pure conscience. Whatever it was, we may be
sure that it was advantageous to Abigail when she encountered
David by the mountainside. However, there is no indication
that she was aware of her beauty or that she used it as a
crutch.

2. *She had an understanding heart.*

The Bible says that Abigail was a woman of good understanding. There is no elaboration upon this, but as the story
unfolds, we see very clearly what is meant by the statement.
She understood human nature. She knew what to expect from
an evil, drunken man like Nabal and was not at all surprised
to learn of his insult to David. She knew it was futile to rebuke him for his drunkenness or his bad behavior. She was
quick to recognize the contrast between the churlish Nabal
and the impetuous David. She knew that impetuosity often
hides a soft heart, and she had faith in David's inherent
goodness. Perhaps she even knew that a few words of praise
would go a long way in softening his attitude toward those
who had done him evil.

3. *She possessed great wisdom.*

Wisdom and good understanding may be closely related,
but not necessarily synonomous. One may possess good understanding of why people do thus and so, or why certain actions
may be expected from certain people, yet lack the wisdom to
make good decisions relative to their own lives. Conversely,
one may have a great amount of knowledge and yet lack the
understanding of how to use that knowledge. Solomon gave
us a proverb which helps us to understand the relationship
between these two characteristics: "Wisdom is the principal
thing; therefore get wisdom: and with all thy getting get
understanding" (Proverbs 4:7). By coupling these two virtues, Abigail was able to divert tragedy from her home and
family.

4. *She exercised prudence.*

Prudence is the ability to regulate and discipline oneself
through the exercise of reason; or it may mean skill or

sagacity in the management of one's affairs. Had Nabal been sober, he might have been prudent enough to understand that an insult to a man of David's reputation was an open invitation for trouble; but since drunkenness destroys one's reasoning ability, he acted foolishly. Abigail had no choice but to take the situation in hand, or perish. This she did skillfully, thus compensating for the lack of her husband's good judgment.

5. *She was a woman of action.*

A decision is of no effect unless it is acted upon. For the most part, people are remembered for their deeds rather than their words. Action makes history, for history is the record of events. Had not Abigail taken action, she would never have been recorded in sacred history as one who influenced a mighty king to desist from a dishonorable deed.

7. *She was a peacemaker.*

A state of war existed between the camp of David and the household of Nabal. It was only the timely intervention of a courageous woman that prevented bloodshed. In reviewing the life and deeds of David, it would appear to us, in our modern understanding of moral values, that David many times was guilty of the shedding of innocent blood. On this one occasion, at least, he was prevented from such an act by the plea of a righteous woman.

8. *Humility was one of her chief virtues.*

When the opportunity came for Abigail to become the wife of the great and honored David, she felt unworthy. She first exhibited humility when she fell upon her face before David and conversed with him in the wilderness. It could be said, and true enough, that humility is a necessity when one is pleading for his life. Abigail's humility before David may have sprung from her knowledge that he was chosen of God to be the ruler of His people. Who could face God in arrogance? Who could face God's anointed in any manner but a humble one? Certainly not Abigail, for she was a truly devout woman.

9. *She was a good organizer.*

The manner in which Abigail went about the preparation, packing, and loading of the food, and her instructions to the servants, bear testimony to her organizational ability. She went about the job as if she had had months in which to prepare for it, yet the urgency of the situation demanded that it be done in only a few hours. Abigail's speech to David was perfect in its organization. Let us look at it in outline form:

1. Exhibition of humility.
2. Apology for her husband's rudeness.
3. Presentation of the requested food.
4. Praise of David's service to God.
5. Assurance of God's continued blessings for him.
6. Plea for her household.

10. *She was a trustworthy counselor.*

All of the above characteristics are a combination which made Abigail a capable adviser, even to a king. David probably called upon her many times for her superior advice and thanked God many times for sending her to him, even as he did that first time he met her: "Blessed be the Lord God of Israel, which sent thee this day to meet me" (1 Samuel 25:32).

In a Nutshell

1. Living up to his name, which means "fool," Nabal indulged in drink, turned a deaf ear to a just call for help, returned evil for good, and insulted the Lord's anointed.

2. A beautiful countenance may be an asset to a woman, but it alone is not sufficient for meeting life's problems. It must be backed by integrity and purity of purpose.

3. The cultivation of an understanding heart is profitable, for it opens the door of confidence in all human relationships; it bridges the gap between husband and wife, parents and children, friends and nations.

4. Wisdom, understanding, and prudence are similar virtues, yet they complement each other.

5. True wisdom is based upon knowledge of God, for the Scripture says, "The fear of the Lord is the beginning of knowledge" (Proverbs 1:7).

6. "Blessed are the peacemakers: for they shall be called the children of God" (Matthew 5:9).

7. Many a worthy cause has been lost for lack of good organization followed by immediate action.

8. The ability to make the right decisions quickly is a mark of maturity.

9. When in need of advice, seek counsel from one who is understanding of heart, wise in the ways of the Lord, humble in spirit, and prudent in action.

Discussion

1. What virtue is there in a wife's remaining with a husband who is churlish, drunken, and evil in all his ways?

2. Is it necessary that a person be superior in knowledge and experience in order to give good advice?

3. When and how does God recompense the righteous and punish the evil?

Closing Prayer

We humble ourselves before Thee, O God, in gratefulness for Thy tender mercies and good gifts to us. May we ever seek Thy guiding hand as we reach toward perfection in our devotion to Thee and in our service in Thy church. In all our dealings with our fellow men, may we exhibit wisdom and prudence so that Thy name may be glorified. We pray through the blessed name of our Lord Jesus. Amen.

The Leader's Notes

Chapter VII

MARY, THE MOTHER OF JESUS

Scripture Background for Study: Matthew 1, 2; 12:46-50; Mark 6:3; Luke 1, 2; John 2:1-12; 19:25-27; Acts 1: 13, 14

Song Selections: 1. "All Hail the Power of Jesus' Name"
2. "'Tis So Sweet to Trust in Jesus"
3. "Take Time to Be Holy" (*prayer hymn*)

Prayer Period

Scripture Reading: Luke 1:39-56

The Bible Story

Approximately four hundred years after God's last visit to His people through the prophets, the New Testament opens with the incarnation of God's only begotten Son as the fulfillment of His most precious promise to His creatures. The prophets had said that He would be born of a virgin (Isaiah 7:14) in the city of Bethlehem (Micah 5:2), and that He would come of the line of David (Isaiah 9:7).

During the time when Israel was under the yoke of Rome, in the days of King Herod, there lived in Nazareth of Galilee, a young Hebrew maiden by the name of Mary. She was engaged to be married to Joseph, a man of the house of David and a carpenter by trade. The reasons that this particular girl was so highly favored in being chosen to become the mother of our Lord are not obvious to us. In the days when the faith of God's people fed upon the promise of a coming Messiah, there must have been many a maiden whose heart burned with an anxious hope, and perhaps a secret dread, that she might be the one singled out for that highest of all honors. Probably there were many true daughters of Abraham, whose beautiful examples of piety and purity qualified them for the honor, yet Mary was the one chosen.

The angel Gabriel appeared to Mary with the message

that she would conceive and bring forth a son who would be called "the Son of the Highest" and who would reign forever upon the throne of David (Luke 1:28-33). Perplexed by this announcement and not understanding such an unprecedented event, she asked, "How shall this be, seeing I know not a man?" (Luke 1:34). Whereupon, the angel assured her that this thing was of God, since all things are possible with Him, and that the child would be truly the promised Messiah, begotten of God. He also informed her that her cousin Elisabeth had conceived in her old age and was now in the sixth month of her pregnancy.

Without revealing to anyone the message she had received from the angel—as far as we can tell—Mary made haste to go the three days' journey into the hill country to visit Elisabeth. What a wealth of knowledge and sweet communion these two women shared during Mary's three months' visit! It was during this visit that Mary uttered the lofty and inspired words of the Magnificat, which for beauty and sublimity is not surpassed by the most renowned poets of Israel. Some have considered it a farewell specimen of Hebrew poetry—the last psalm of Jewish inspiration. In it we can sense the outrush of a pure and grateful heart. Its tone is that of joy and exultation, marked by the deepest humility.

Upon her return to Nazareth, Mary was faced with the serious problem of Joseph's reaction to her condition, and the social implications involved. Joseph did, indeed, doubt her fidelity and determined to "put her away privily" (Matthew 1:19), which was the kindest and most honorable treatment he could give to the woman whom he truly loved. Conscious of her innocence, Mary offered no defense, no plea, but calmly resolved to leave her fate to her God, who had already taken her cause into His own hands. This unhappy state of affairs was relieved by a message from God, which upheld Mary's integrity and revealed to Joseph that she was to become the mother of the long-awaited Messiah (Matthew 1:20). Joseph immediately took her as his wife, and thus became the protector of Mary and the holy child.

The events of the nativity are so well known to Christians that we need not dwell upon them in detail here. This is a character study of Mary as a woman, and our main concern is her reaction to these wonderful events. We have only one statement from the Scripture which gives us any enlightenment: "But Mary kept all these things, and pondered them in her heart" (Luke 2:19). Although she was well acquainted with the Old Testament teaching regarding these events, Mary did not fully comprehend the magnitude and scope of Christ's advent. Her emotions were strange, mixed, and unutterable. Gazing upon the face and form of her first-born son, she experienced the same sublime joy any mother knows at such a time, yet awe and reverence mingled with the deep maternal impulses of her heart.

The life of the precious babe was nourished, protected, and guided through the years of infancy, childhood, and early youth. We have every reason to believe that it was a perfectly normal life that He led and that Mary was a normal mother, facing all the normal problems of child care. Only one incident is given in the Gospel record which is relative to these years. That is the story of Jesus' experience with the learned doctors in the temple when He was twelve years old (Luke 2:41-52). This story relates that His mother gently rebuked Him for bringing anxiety to their hearts. His answer, "wist ye not that I must be about my Father's business?" (verse 49) proves that He was always aware of His deity and His mission upon the earth. Yet, as a proper child should, He obeyed Mary and Joseph, and was subject to them until He became a full-grown man.

Let us again emphasize the fact that Mary was unaware of the full significance of the coming of the Christ child, for on this occasion the record says regarding Mary and Joseph, "they understood not the saying which he spake unto them" (verse 50). And again the statement is made that Mary "kept all these sayings in her heart" (verse 51). Any other normal mother would do the same thing under like circumstances.

This incident in the boyhood of Jesus closes with the summarizing statement: "And Jesus increased in wisdom and stature, and in favour with God and man" (verse 52). This indicates that He was a perfectly normal boy in every respect, for this statement could truthfully be made of any average boy, who was blessed with wise and godly parents.

The next scene in which Mary appears in relation to Jesus is at the marriage feast in Cana of Galilee (John 2:1-11). This took place early in His public career and is called the "beginning of miracles" (verse 11). At this affair, Mary participated in a small way in the happenings of the day. The next verse following this incident states that Jesus' mother, His brothers, and His disciples accompanied Him to Capernaum where they tarried a few days. Three of the Gospel writers state that on one occasion, in the midst of one of His public discourses, Mary and His brothers appeared and wished to speak with Him (Matthew 12:46-50; Mark 3:31-35; Luke 8:19-21).

All of these events prove that Mary kept in close contact with Jesus during the years of His public ministry and that her faith in Him remained undaunted. She was His first disciple, and worshiped Him as God, while she cherished Him as her son.

In the closing scenes of His earthly life, when He was scorned by the world, forsaken by His closest friends, and judged worthy of death by the courts, both religious and civil, she did not desert Him. One of the seven sayings of Jesus while He hung upon the cross was a statement relative to His mother. Seeing her standing at the foot of the cross, He looked upon her and said, "Woman, behold thy son!" (John 19:26). Then He looked at John and said, "Behold thy mother!" (John 19:27). The same verse further states that from that hour on John took her into his own home. Many scholars think that Mary was a widow by this time and was in need of a home after the death of Jesus.

While the Gospel writers have nothing to say of Mary during the events after the resurrection and before the ascension, it seems natural to suppose that she saw Him and conversed with Him. We know nothing of her feelings at this time, but these startling events must have brought to her a new understanding of her mission. The consciousness of her motherhood waned as she became more acutely aware of the divine sonship of Jesus.

Only one other time is Mary mentioned and that is a reference to her presence, along with the eleven apostles and certain other women, in the upper room, where they had met for prayer and supplication (Acts 1:13, 14). This was after the ascension and before the establishment of the church on the Day of Pentecost. Because of her belief in Jesus as the Saviour of the world, we believe that she was a faithful worker in the early church. However, since no further mention is made of her, there is no particular reason to believe that she had prominence above any other faithful Christian woman.

Character Analysis

Mary is the most difficult of all outstanding Bible women to characterize. This is true for two reasons:

1. All that is said of her is in relationship to Jesus, and since He is the central figure of all history, the long-promised Messiah, God incarnate, any interest in Mary naturally slips far into the background in the Scriptural narrative. The Gospel writers were not concerned about preserving a picture or description of Mary for posterity. They were vitally intent on presenting Jesus as the only begotten Son of God and the Saviour of the world.

2. The many traditions that have grown up through the years regarding the person and mission of Mary confuse the average person. In trying to evaluate tradition, we must check carefully what the Bible has to say about the subject. What the Bible does *not* say may be more revealing. Nowhere in the Bible is Mary said to be holy; she was not worshiped or adored. The Wise-men came to worship the child, not the mother (Matthew 2:11). There is no record that the early church recognized Mary in any special sense, either while she lived or after her death. Nowhere does the Bible speak of her as a mediator or intercessor. Paul tells us, "there is one God, and one mediator between God and men, the man Christ Jesus" (1 Timothy 2:5).

Because tradition has obviously created a false view of Mary, there is danger that many may fail to give her the honor that is rightfully hers. In the light of the Scriptures alone, let us try to understand her as a normal woman.

1. *She is the most highly favored woman of all ages.*

We may be sure that the highest favor God had to bestow upon a woman would be given to one whose heart was pure, whose nature was gentle, and whose character was unquestioned. This does not necessarily mean that Mary was incapable of committing sin, or that she actually did live above sin (Romans 3:23; Galatians 3:22).

The angel Gabriel hailed Mary as "thou that art highly favoured" (Luke 1:28). Elizabeth said to her, "Blessed art thou among women" (Luke 1:42), and Mary said of herself, "from henceforth all generations shall call me blessed" (Luke 1:48).

2. *She was true to the divine trust that was given to her.*

Mary had the most important task ever given to a woman: that of the physical care of God's Son. She was faithful to that charge, and with the help of Joseph and the direction of God, brought the child Jesus to full manhood without mishap. The flight into Egypt is one example of the changes the parents were called upon to make for the safety of the child. Mary must have guarded carefully each baby step, each morsel of food, each act in play. Later, both Mary and Joseph watched over Him as He learned the carpenter's trade.

Some have charged the parents with carelessness in regard to the incident in the temple when Jesus was twelve years of age. When the customs of the people and the age are understood, that charge is proven false. The people traveled in great numbers to and from the religious festivals, the adults tending to visit along the way, and the children getting together as children of any age are inclined to do. Mary deserves sympathy and understanding rather than criticism. Any mother who has ever lost a child, even for a few hours, can testify to this.

3. *Mary was a deeply spiritual woman.*

She observed the Mosaic law under which she lived. Her wisdom and spiritual discernment were manifested in the circumcision of her Son, His presentation at the temple, and her own purification forty days after the birth. She listened to the prophecies of Simeon and the aged Anna in the temple, perhaps not comprehending more than a small portion of their meaning. Through the years Mary and Joseph made the customary journeys to the temple for sacrifices and worship. According to the law of Moses, the children in their home were taught about the religion and history of their people. This was done in the home, and, for the boys, in the synagogue school.

4. *She grew in the grace and knowledge of the Lord Jesus.*

This may be a strange statement, but Mary's knowledge of Jesus unfolded gradually with the passing of time and the occurrence of the events in His earthly life. She did not have a complete revelation of Him from the beginning. Simeon's words to Mary, "a sword shall pierce through thy own soul also" (Luke 2: 35), cast a dark and foreboding shadow over her happiness of the moment, yet she did not fully understand the statement until about thirty-three years later.

Like all the other disciples, Mary expected Jesus' realm to be physical—earthly—and one that would exalt the Jews above all other nations. She was well acquainted with the teaching of the prophets regarding Him. She had heard His own teaching regarding the kingdom and she had witnessed many of His miracles, but she still did not understand that His kingdom would be spiritual. It was only after His resurrection that she, along with the other disciples, began to realize the true nature of His kingdom and the reason for His coming to earth.

In a Nutshell

1. Every woman who gives birth to a child has received a trust from God and will some day give an account of her stewardship.

2. It is not strange that Mary "pondered (all these things) ... in her heart," for she must have been one of the loneliest women of the world.

3. Angels are God's messengers, and so are we.

4. The perfect pattern for the development of human personality is fourfold in scope: physical, mental, social, and spiritual. Neglect of any part of this plan results in a warped personality.

5. The ultimate goal of all human behavior should be to find favor with God.

6. Jesus taught that the human family bond is transcended by a stronger bond—that bond of the spirit which makes us all brothers and sisters in Christ (Matthew 12:46-50; Mark 3:31-35; Luke 8:19-21).

7. Since tradition may be true or false, the wisdom of accepting it wholeheartedly is questionable, but who can question what God has revealed through the Holy Scriptures?

MOTHER'S LOVE

Her love is like an island
  In life's ocean, vast and wide,
A peaceful, quiet shelter
  From the wind, the rain, the tide.

'Tis bound on the north by Hope,
  By Patience on the west,
By tender Counsel on the south,
  And on the east by Rest.

Above it like a beacon light
  Shine Faith, and Truth, and Prayer;
And through the changing scenes of life
  I find a haven there.

—Author Unknown

Discussion

1. Can any mother compare her motherhood with the motherhood of Mary?

2. What influence does art, literature, and music exert on our understanding of Mary as a normal human being?

3. Which would be more difficult:

    a. For a mother to see her innocent son executed?
    b. For a mother to see her guilty son executed?

Closing Prayer

Heavenly Father, we thank Thee for Thy revealed Word. We ask Thy guidance as we search for a true picture of Mary, the mother of our Lord. May our study help us to understand the highest meaning of motherhood and to accept more graciously its responsibilities. Help us to grow in the grace and knowledge of our Lord Jesus Christ, so that others may witness His radiance and beauty shining through each deed and thought of our lives. In His name we pray, Amen.

The Leader's Notes

CHAPTER VIII

MARTHA, A MISUNDERSTOOD WOMAN

SCRIPTURE BACKGROUND FOR STUDY: Luke 10: 38-42; John 11: 1-46; 12: 1-9

SONG SELECTIONS:
1. "What a Friend We Have in Jesus"
2. "All the Way My Saviour Leads Me"
3. "Jesus Calls Us" (*prayer hymn*)

PRAYER PERIOD

SCRIPTURE READING: Luke 10: 38-42

The Bible Story

In human weakness we often tend to forget all that is good about a person and remember only the bad. Martha, who tenderly ministered to the physical needs of Jesus on numerous occasions, is remembered by many people only as a woman who was once rebuked by Jesus. Because her sense of values became a little confused, she has become one of the most misunderstood women of the Bible.

Martha, Mary, and Lazarus lived in the obscure little village of Bethany about two miles from Jerusalem on the southeastern slope of the Mount of Olives. It was to this quiet and peaceful home, where love and sympathy held sway, that Jesus often retired for sustenance and rest from toil and travel. Jesus once said of himself, "The foxes have holes, and the birds of the air have nests; but the Son of man hath not where to lay his head" (Matthew 8:20); yet in this home He always found a welcome. If anywhere on earth He may be said to have had a home, it was with these three who were devoted to Him. Many and touching are the incidents which illustrate their great love for the Son of God.

There is evidence to believe that this home was a home of considerable means, for the entertainment of Jesus and those who traveled with Him was far too expensive for a poor family to undertake. The precious ointment which Mary poured on the feet of Jesus on one occasion indicates that this was a family that possessed substantial wealth (John 12:3).

The first mention we have of this family is on the occasion of a visit from Jesus. In amiable sweetness and gentle submission, Mary sat at the feet of Jesus to drink from the fountain of His love and wisdom. Martha's sense of responsibility and awareness of His physical needs constrained her to make haste in the preparation of a great feast, which she felt was necessary. In her anxiety for perfection as a hostess, she forgot the importance of feeding the hunger of the human heart, and asked that Jesus bid Mary help her with the serving.

His answer was gentle, but effective: "Martha, Martha, thou art careful and troubled about many things: but one thing is needful: and Mary hath chosen that good part, which shall not be taken away from her" (Luke 10:41, 42). On the strength of this one rebuke, many have censured Martha as being irritable, worldly, and socially ambitious. It is true that Mary's spiritual sight was keener and her heart more in tune with the words of life as they fell from the lips of the Master, yet there is no indication that Jesus meant to condemn Martha for spiritual coldness. Rather, it seems that He was reminding her that the fretting and anxiety she exhibited over the serving of a meal, which would be forgotten tomorrow, were robbing her of an opportunity to partake of an infinitely greater repast. This feast, when partaken of, would satisfy the hunger of her very soul. There are few women today who do not need constant reminders of this great truth.

The next incident regarding this family relates one of the Bible's most unforgettable stories—the raising of Lazarus from the dead. When Lazarus became ill, the sisters sent for Jesus, but Lazarus died and had been buried four days before Jesus arrived. When Martha heard that Jesus was coming, she went a good distance from the town to meet Him. She poured out her grief to Him and affirmed her belief that God would do whatever He asked.

Jesus said to her, "I am the resurrection, and the life: he that believeth in me, though he were dead, yet shall he live: and whosoever liveth and believeth in me shall never die. Believest thou this?" (John 11:25, 26). These memorable words, first spoken to Martha, have comforted millions through the centuries and are among the most cherished words of Jesus.

Martha's answer, "Yea, Lord: I believe that thou art the Christ, the Son of God, which should come into the world" (John 11: 27), is the most magnificent confession of faith which can be uttered by mortal tongue.

While this was taking place, Mary had remained within the house. As the party drew near, Martha hastened secretly into the house to call her sister, saying that the Master wished to see her. When Mary met Him, she fell at His feet and cried, "Lord, if thou hadst been here, my brother had not died" (John 11: 32)—the very same words that Martha had spoken a little earlier.

Then follows one of the most touching scenes in the life of Jesus. When He saw Mary and the people who had gathered around, all weeping because of the death of Lazarus, His great heart was moved in sympathy and the fountain of His tears overflowed. The record says simply, "Jesus wept" (John 11: 35). This is the shortest verse in the Bible, yet what a great story of love and compassion it tells!

Jesus commanded that the stone be rolled away from the tomb. When Martha protested because Lazarus had been so long dead, Jesus said to her, "Said I not unto thee, that, if thou wouldest believe, thou shouldest see the glory of God?" (John 11: 40). Then He prayed and commanded Lazarus to come forth from the grave. Martha did, indeed, see the glory of God, for immediately her brother stepped from the grave, dressed still in his burial robes. What a moment this was! Lazarus, whom all knew to have been dead and in the tomb four days, was resurrected and completely restored to his former good health. Though Mary and Martha were poles apart in temperament, they were one in spirit as they received their brother back into the bosom of the family.

The third and final scene in which Mary and Martha appeared took place six days before the last Passover feast. Jesus came to Bethany and stopped with these friends. The pattern is much the same as on His former visit: Martha served the meal, while Mary took "a pound of ointment of spikenard, very costly, and anointed the feet of Jesus, and wiped his feet with her hair: and the house was filled with the odour of the ointment" (John 12:3).

The pouring of fragrant ointments upon the head or the feet of honored guests at a banquet was the customary procedure, but Mary had a much deeper motive than mere adherence to social patterns. Hers was an act of love performed upon the person of the Saviour of the world. Again, she was commended by Jesus for her devotion, for when Judas protested the waste of such costly perfume, He said, "Let her alone: against the day of my burying hath she kept this" (John 12:7).

Now for a final glimpse of Martha. What was she thinking while this touching scene was taking place? Was she still so "cumbered about much serving" (Luke 10:40) that she was unaware of Mary's act? Probably not. More than likely she stood close by, sanctioning Mary's lavish use of the costly perfume. This time she did not chide or complain, for she had come to accept her sister's seeming indifference to the responsibility of running a household. She knew that Mary's indifference was apparent, only because of her preoccupation with spiritual matters. Jesus had said that was the "good part" which should not be taken away from her.

Although Mary and Martha were opposite types in every way, they each had their own special way of serving Jesus, and He loved them both. Martha had a blessed privilege in receiving Jesus into her home, and should be remembered because of her many acts of love and devotion to Him.

Character Analysis

1. *She was an attentive hostess.*

One of the most complimentary statements that can be made about a woman is that she is a gracious hostess. Martha loved to entertain, and what a privilege she had in receiving the heavenly Guest into her home! She delighted in serving Him a tasty and sumptuous feast. She took care that His every physical need was provided for in a most generous manner. Had not Jesus detected her anxiety over these unnecessary services, she might have missed a great spiritual feast at His table.

2. *She was an industrious housekeeper.*

A well-kept home is a delight to any family. It is commendable that Martha was proud of her home and took great pains to keep it orderly and clean. The wise Solomon said of the virtuous woman, ''She looketh well to the ways of her household, and eateth not the bread of idleness'' (Proverbs 31:27). These words fit Martha, just as if they were written specifically for her.

3. *She was practical-minded.*

The natural bent of Martha's disposition was toward industrious activity, practical to the last degree. Had this not been so, there might have been a fast for her guests instead of a feast. On the occasion of the death of Lazarus, she could not wait for Jesus to reach the house, but hurried away to meet Him. Her grief was very real and she had to *do* something about it. By contrast, Mary's grief struck her down, like a wounded thing, immobile and defenseless.

4. *She maintained strong family ties.*

This closely knit family affords the best glimpse we have of family life during the personal ministry of Jesus. They were in full sympathy with the mission of Jesus, and His frequent visits strengthened the ties that bound their hearts to each other in beautiful harmony and affection. To Martha goes much of the credit for setting family standards. Her strong personality and practical mind were the balance wheel which regulated family relationships.

5. *She had great spiritual discernment.*

Despite Mary's anointing of Jesus with the precious perfume and drying His feet with her hair, and despite her choice of that better part in her devotion to Jesus, it was with Martha that He discussed the profound subject of life after death. It was Martha who made the good confession, even as did Peter at Caesarea Philippi, "thou art the Christ, the Son of God" (John 11:27). It was Martha who expressed her belief that God would do whatever Jesus asked. This is not meant to discredit Mary, but rather to defend Martha because she is often looked upon as having been indifferent to spiritual things.

6. *She was responsive to the teaching of Jesus.*

Much of the teaching of Jesus fell upon deaf ears. At one time He said, "their ears are dull of hearing, and their eyes they have closed" (Matthew 13:15). Not so of Martha! She not only listened eagerly to His teaching, but her heart was quick to understand. How else would she have known that Lazarus would "rise again in the resurrection at the last day" (John 11:24)?

Martha was teachable. It has been said that there is no teaching unless there is learning. After Martha was rebuked by Jesus for confusing her sense of values, we do not hear of her making that same mistake again. It would be a beautiful world indeed if everyone responded to Jesus' teaching in this manner.

In a Nutshell

1. "Despise not thou the chastening of the Lord, nor faint when thou art rebuked of him: for whom the Lord loveth he chasteneth" (Hebrews 12:5, 6).

2. Good housekeeping is important, but not as important as good "soul-keeping."

3. Every Christian woman should be an attentive hostess to Christ, the unseen Guest in her home.

4. Jesus, the bread of heaven, satisfies the hunger of the human heart. Which will you have, a feast or a fast?

5. Family ties in a Christian home are not broken by physical death, but by spiritual death.

6. A little adversity often acts as a good hearing aid for those whose spiritual ears are dull of hearing.

Discussion

1. Do most modern-day women have a greater feeling of kinship with Mary or with Martha?

2. Why are people inclined to hold one fault against a person when there are many virtues to remember?

3. Have you ever wondered why Lazarus had nothing to say of his experience in the resurrection from the dead?

Closing Prayer

Loving Father, we thank Thee for the beautiful story of Mary and Martha, and for the inspiration that comes to us from a study of these two truly devoted women. Because physical things are so easily seen, we often let our spiritual eyes stray from that good part of sitting at the feet of Jesus. Help us to be strong in faith so that our sense of values may not become confused. In the name of Jesus we pray. Amen.

The Leader's Notes

Chapter IX

SALOME, THE AMBITIOUS MOTHER

Scripture Background for Study: Matthew 20:20-28; 27:
56; Mark 1:19, 20; 10:35-45; 15:40

Song Selections: 1. "Must Jesus Bear the Cross Alone?"
2. "The Way of the Cross Leads Home"
3. "O Master, Let Me Walk With Thee"
(prayer hymn)

Prayer Period

Scripture Reading: Matthew 20:20-28

The Bible Story

The Gospel writers mention very few women who crossed the path of Jesus during His public ministry. Next to His own mother, Salome is the most conspicuous mother mentioned. What we know of her is very little, and is told in only a few scattered verses, yet a great lesson can be drawn from this meager account.

Matthew identifies her as the mother of Zebedee's children (20:20), while Mark gives us her name, Salome (15:40; 16:1) and identifies Zebedee's children as James and John (10:35). Zebedee was a fisherman by trade and lived on the shore of the Sea of Galilee, probably near Capernaum. He must have been a man of considerable means, for he had servants who attended to his ship.

One day, while James and John were in the boat with their father, Jesus came by and called them to be His apostles. Immediately, they left the fishing nets which they had been mending and followed Him (Mark 1:19, 20). With the passing of time, these two young fishermen, along with Peter, became known as the "inner circle" of Jesus' disciples, for it seems that He had a special feeling of warmth for these three, and they for Him. When Jesus was transfigured upon the mountain, it was only these three who witnessed this momentous scene. Again, they went with Him farther into the

78

garden of Gethsemane than the others. John seems to have been especially aware of this bond, for in his Gospel he always refers to himself as "that disciple whom Jesus loved."

One day, not long before the crucifixion, Salome asked a very special favor of Jesus. He had been telling the twelve about His approaching death and subsequent resurrection. They supposed this would be the time when He would begin His reign over an earthly kingdom. He had previously told them that when the time came for Him to sit upon His throne of glory, they, the twelve apostles, would sit upon twelve thrones, judging the twelve tribes of Israel (Matthew 19:28).

With these things in mind, Salome, hoping to be first with such a request, came to Jesus with her sons, and bowing before Him, asked that He give James and John a place of honor in His kingdom—one to sit on His right hand and the other on His left hand (Matthew 20:21). We must note here that Mark indicates that it was James and John who made the request (Mark 10:35-40), ignoring altogether the mother's part, or even her presence. Considering both accounts, it is difficult to tell in whose mind the idea first sprang up, but there is no room for doubting Salome's ambition to see her sons occupying prominent places of honor in the new kingdom. Were they not already closer to Him than the others? Why not take steps to assure this same association with Him in the kingdom to come?

Jesus' answer seems to be directed toward James and John: "Ye know not what ye ask. Are ye able to drink of the cup that I shall drink of, and to be baptized with the baptism that I am baptized with?" (Matthew 20:22). He was speaking of His coming agony to Gethsemane as He wrestled with himself, and the weary trudge up Calvary's mountain to His crucifixion.

Their request was based upon faith and ignorance—faith that He would indeed have a kingdom, but ignorance in believing it would be an earthly kingdom. Ignorance was again apparent in their prompt reply to His question: "We are able" (Matthew 20:22). They were totally unaware of the meaning of the way of the cross, the way of suffering, but they were later to learn the significance of these mysteries.

Jesus assured them that they would indeed become partakers of His suffering, and as we follow their stories to the end we see how true this prediction was. James was the first of the twelve to spill his blood and thus seal his testimony for Christ. He was beheaded by Herod (Acts 12:1, 2). John's suffering was in a vastly different manner. He was exiled to the Isle of Patmos, where, though he lived bodily, he was deprived of his personal testimony for Christ. Yet, while in exile, he received the last word from Jesus, which he recorded. It is preserved for us in the book of Revelation. Thus his final testimony has reached through the centuries as a blessed assurance that a crown of life awaits all those who remain faithful until death (Revelation 2:10).

Finally, Jesus told them that the honors of heaven were not His to give. God alone would decide whose they should be. He followed this by patiently and gently teaching that the way to greatness is not a path of ease, but a path of service— a path of suffering every step of the way. The episode closes with His statement, "Even as the Son of man came not to be ministered unto, but to minister, and to give his life a ransom for many" (Matthew 20:28). In this He did not hesitate to refer to himself as the perfect example His disciples should follow.

We do not know Salome's reaction to Jesus' answer to her request. Perhaps she was more confused than ever regarding the kingdom of heaven. We do know that His refusal to grant her request did not deter her from faithfully ministering to Him until the end, for she was one of the women who followed Him to the cross (Matthew 27:55, 56). She was one of the women who prepared spices and ointments for the burial of His body (Luke 23:55, 56). She was at the empty tomb early on the day of resurrection and heard the announcement of the angel, "He is not here, but is risen" (Luke 24:6). She, along with the other women, was privileged to make the announcement of His resurrection to the apostles (Luke 24:10).

This is the last account we have of Salome. Although not

specifically mentioned, she probably was one of the women who met in the upper room with the apostles immediately after the ascension (Acts 1:14). Considering the faithful service of this devout woman during Jesus' public ministry, especially during the trying hours of the crucifixion and at the tomb, it seems very likely that she was one of the leading women in the early church. Perhaps by this time she fully understood Jesus' teaching regarding true greatness.

Although the main event recorded of Salome's life is one which portrays her in a critical light, we must consider the whole story with all its implications, in order fully to appreciate her. We believe that her good characteristics by far overbalance her one experience in confusing worldly fame with true greatness. We must conclude that she learned a lesson in humility, which sustained her through the succeeding years and opened the door of her heart to a fuller understanding of the kingdom of heaven.

Character Analysis

1. *She maintained a close family relationship.*

Salome's closeness in thought with her sons and her physical presence with them in public places indicate the high esteem they held for her. Many mothers of today, who stand condemned for their failure to maintain a close bond of fellowship within the family, could learn a lesson from Salome. She is one of the New Testament's best examples of a mother who kept the family ties strong and unbroken by discord.

2. *She was a true disciple of Jesus.*

Early in the ministry of Jesus many of His disciples turned back from following Him because of the "hardness" of His teaching (John 6:60, 66). The word disciple means "follower" or "learner." Salome was a true disciple of Jesus —one who did not flinch when the most ambitious desire of her life was denied by Jesus. His teaching on this occasion was especially hard for her to accept because she stood condemned, and publicly, too, for the selfish desire she had for her children. She did not permit one frustrating experience to mar her joy in service for Him, or close her mind to His teaching.

3. *She gave a rich spiritual legacy to her children.*

A truly devout mother always has a deep concern for the spiritual welfare of her children. She leaves nothing to chance in their early training. Salome's closeness in feeling with her sons gave her an opportunity early in their lives to impart to them the right attitudes about the things of the spirit: God, the law of Moses, righteousness, forgiveness, etc. When James and John were called to be Christ's apostles, she was wholly sympathetic with the idea, for her own training was good preparation for such an event.

4. *She remained faithful to Jesus until the end.*

We do not have a record of the beginning of Salome's discipleship, but it likely began at the time James and John were called to be His apostles. We know that it continued until His ascension, and we have every reason to believe that she remained faithful until her own death. In this she exhibited a spiritual fortitude which should be admired and emulated by all. Jesus could have commended her for this—perhaps did—for on one occasion He taught, ''No man, having put his hand to the plow, and looking back, is fit for the kingdom of God'' (Luke 9:62).

5. *She was ambitious for her children.*

Salome should not be criticized too severely because she mistook worldly position for true greatness. This is an error of judgment which is a constant threat to Christ's followers even today when we have a much broader concept of the kingdom of heaven. She and her two sons were not alone in this spiritually unhealthy desire, for the other ten were angry with James and John when they learned of their request. This is an indication that they each desired the same honor, but had been outmaneuvered. On other occasions, the twelve had disputed about which of them would be greatest in the kingdom (Mark 9:34; Luke 22:24).

We must not conclude that Salome's misguided ambition for her sons was the basis for her own discipleship. Her love for Christ was genuine, and she followed Him because she believed Him to be the Messiah, even as He claimed to be.

In a Nutshell

1. If we understand the events recorded in the Bible, we must look upon the people involved as being ordinary human beings who were subjected to extraordinary happenings and the most extraordinary personality.

2. A mother's ambition for her children should be based upon service, not worldly honor; sacrifice, not worldly gain; work, not worldly pleasure.

3. The petitions of many Christians today could be answered just as Jesus answered Salome: "Ye know not what ye ask" (Matthew 20:22).

4. The way of the cross leads home.

5. He who lacks the grace to bear the cross deserves not the glory of wearing the crown.

6. If Christianity is worth anything, it is worth everything.

7. A mother's misguided ambition for her children can result in their complete estrangement from God.

8. Our hope for eternal life is secured by Christ who lived as a servant, died as a sacrifice, arose as a conqueror, and ascended as a king.

Discussion

1. Is a mother's ambition for her children to occupy places of prominence in government, in business, in professions, or in social circles ever justified?

2. How much satisfaction is there in accepting a place of honor which is undeserved?

3. Is this story suggestive of modern political maneuvering?

Closing Prayer

Heavenly Father, we thank Thee for this lesson on humility, and pray that we may ever be on guard lest we fall into the error of desiring undue honor for ourselves. Help us to realize that the lowest seat in heaven is well worth all the effort we put forth to live Christlike lives here on earth. Walk with us day by day as we travel the road of service, sacrifice, and love that leads to that heavenly home where we shall wear a crown and reign with Christ forever. In His name we pray. Amen.

The Leader's Notes

CHAPTER X

DORCAS, A WOMAN FULL OF GOOD WORKS

SCRIPTURE BACKGROUND FOR STUDY: Acts 9:36-42
SONG SELECTIONS: 1. "Is Your Life a Channel of Blessing?"
                 2. "While the Days Are Going By"
                 3. "Let Him Have His Way With Thee"
                   (*prayer hymn*)
PRAYER PERIOD
SCRIPTURE READING: Acts 9:36-42

The Bible Story

True benevolence, as it is practiced by Christian people in modern times, was totally unknown until the coming of Christ. The law of Moses made certain provisions for the poor. At the end of every third year a tithe was laid by for the Levites, the strangers, the widows, and the orphans (Deuteronomy 14:28, 29). A residue of all crops, both grain and fruit, was left in the fields for the poor to gather (Leviticus 19:9, 10). Every seventh year was a year of release for the poor, wherein debts were cancelled and bond servants were released and presented with a just portion of the flocks and herds and wine from the winepress (Deuteronomy 15:1-14). Every fiftieth year was a year of jubilee, wherein all bond servants were released and all alienated lands restored (Leviticus 25). This procedure kept a pretty fair balance between the rich and the poor, but it was done by law and not by conscience.

In all the teaching of Jesus very little is said about the good works of looking after the poor and needy, yet Jesus himself is often described as one who had compassion on the multitudes (Matthew 9:36; Mark 5:19). Always He went about doing good. The power of His perfect example in this was felt in the early days of the church and perhaps more so today.

While we cannot find that Jesus made specific regulations for the care of the needy, we do find the early church practicing benevolence towards the widows, orphans, and all the saints who were in need (Acts 2:45; 4:34-37). We must conclude that this practice was an outgrowth of the teaching of Christ and His apostles. It was done because the love of Christ, abiding in the hearts of His followers, constrained them to love the brethren, and thus take care of those who were not able to care for themselves. The principle of doing good works, with love as the chief motive, is far different from doing good works because the law demands it.

In all the pages of the New Testament, Dorcas is the most outstanding example of an individual who was concerned about the poor and needy. She lived at Joppa, a Mediterranean seaport town about thirty-eight miles northwest of Jerusalem. This city had a large population which depended upon the sea for a living. Because poor equipment and rough seas made fishing a treacherous business, there were many widows and fatherless children living in and near Joppa.

Day by day, Dorcas may have watched these poverty-stricken people comb the beach for bits of clothing and other useful items cast ashore by the sea. Her loving heart was moved with compassion, and she set to work doing what she could to relieve suffering humanity. Using her talent for sewing, she made numerous garments and distributed them among the needy people. We do not know whether Dorcas was a wealthy woman or not, but she must have given generously of her money and time to this project.

One day Dorcas became ill, amid her labors, and died rather suddenly. The disciples in the town gathered in her home, many of them widows whom Dorcas had helped. In deep mourning for their departed benefactress, they prepared her for burial and placed her in an upper room. Immediately, they decided to send for Peter, who was in Lydda about twelve miles away. We cannot be sure just why Peter's presence was desired, but it likely was because Dorcas was a much-loved woman, one who was an important influence in the church at Joppa, and the disciples merely desired the comfort and assurance which they knew Peter could give. It was not customary for the apostles to restore life to deceased brethren or sisters merely because they were beloved or useful in the church. Had that been true, Stephen most certainly would have been raised and restored to the church.

Peter went with the two men who had come for him, and when they reached Joppa, went immediately to the upper chamber. There were the widows standing by, weeping and showing the various garments Dorcas had made for them. Peter asked them all to leave the room, possibly because he wished a closer communion with the Almighty in the prayer he was about to offer. The words of his prayer are not recorded, but at the close of the prayer he turned to the body and said simply, "Tabitha, arise" (Acts 9:40). When she opened her eyes, she saw Peter and sat up. He took her by the hand and presented her alive to the saints and widows. Here the story ends. The scene of rejoicing, the look of awe upon the faces of the mourners, the incredulity, the hurry to spread abroad this amazing incident are all left to the imagination of the reader.

What was the purpose of this miracle, the first of its kind performed by the disciples? The answer lies in the result, for "it was known throughout all Joppa; and many believed in the Lord" (Acts 9:42). Thus Joppa, a field "white unto harvest," became the center of many days of preaching and teaching for Peter.

A glance at the fearful odds against which the early church had to struggle will help us understand this miracle. The church, made up of a weak and unlearned handful of men and women, was destitute of material resources but abounded in faith. She had to contend with impregnable religious prejudices, worldly wisdom, powerful material resources, and political powers with authority to persecute dissenting factions by the sword. A miracle, such as raising a prominent woman from death, was a much needed reinforcement for the struggling little band of Christians.

In meditating upon this story, we wish we knew more about this good woman, both before the marvel of her resurrection and afterward. We have very little information about her as a person or about her private life and family associations. Her name, Tabitha, is an Aramaic word which means antelope or gazelle. Dorcas is the Greek form of the same name. It was customary in that country to name girl babies after some beautiful and graceful animal. Limited though this information is, we can have a wonderful feeling of communion with Dorcas, for her good works are an everlasting testimony to her good character. Jesus said, "by their fruits ye shall know them" (Matthew 7:20).

Perhaps more church groups, as well as social service groups, are named after this industrious woman of the early church than for any other person. The Dorcas Sewing Societies, which are world-wide, are an outgrowth of the spirit of Dorcas, as she ministered to the needs of the poor.

Nothing more is recorded of her after her resurrection, but it is evident that her witness for Christ was increased by this miracle. The poor whom she had befriended and helped now saw in her the embodiment of their own hope of a resurrected body and eternal life in heaven.

Doing good works with love, not law, as the motivation principle, is one of the basic ideas of Christianity. Wherever the teaching of Christ has spread, benevolent and social welfare enterprises have quickly sprung up and flourished. Organization toward good works and institutionalized benevolence were unknown until the coming of Christ. It is the love of Christ living in the hearts of His followers that constrains them to serve Him in this manner. It is an acknowledgment of His teaching, "Inasmuch as ye have done it unto one of the least of these my brethren, ye have done it unto me" (Matthew 25:40).

Character Analysis

1. *She was compassionate.*

One of the most Christlike virtues which can be manifested by a human being is a compassionate heart. When Jesus went about from village to village teaching and healing, He looked upon the multitudes and "was moved with compassion on them, because they fainted, and were scattered abroad, as sheep having no shepherd" (Matthew 9:36). In the same manner, Dorcas could look down from her home high upon the rocky ledge above the shore upon the poor of the city, as they struggled for a morsel of bread or a bit of rags to cover their bodies. She, too, was moved with a feeling of pity for suffering humanity. The Lord concluded His observation by saying, "The harvest truly is plenteous, but the labourers are few" (Matthew 9:37). His compassion was not only for the physical suffering of the people, but also for their spiritual suffering. He asked that the disciples pray to God, the Lord of harvest, to send forth laborers into the field that men and women might be brought into the kingdom.

2. *She was benevolent.*

True compassion leads one to take action. When the throngs of crippled, blind, and diseased people gathered around Jesus, He felt compassion for them and healed them, one and all. In the same manner, the pity Dorcas felt for the underprivileged people of her community led her to take whatever action was necessary, what she was capable of doing to relieve their distress.

When Jesus pictured the last judgment scene to His disciples, He clearly taught that good works, performed for the benefit of the brethren, are the basis upon which each individual will be judged. On this occasion He said, "Inasmuch as ye have done it unto one of the least of these my brethren, ye have done it unto me" (Matthew 25:40). All who perform such good works in the name of Jesus will receive a just reward. "For God is not unrighteous to forget your work and labour of love, which ye have shewed toward his name, in that ye have ministered to the saints" (Hebrews 6:10).

3. *She was industrious.*

Dorcas probably was wealthy enough to satisfy her feeling of compassion for the needy widows by giving money for their support. This would have been an acceptable procedure, but, being industrious and diligent, Dorcas desired to give of herself along with her material aid. The record says she was "full of good works and almsdeeds which she did" (Acts

9:36). This indicates that she was constantly at the job—not satisfied to sit idle for a moment when people all around her were in need. There were no sewing machines in those days, so every garment had to be made by hand. What a tedious and painstaking task she had!

4. *She was unselfish.*

There is no doubt that Dorcas could have been the best dressed woman in all Joppa had she chosen to be. With her gift for sewing and her financial resources, she could have clothed herself in beauty. It would certainly be no mark against her if she dressed attractively. Drabness is not necessarily next to godliness. But because she was a woman professing godliness, she was remembered for her good works, not because she may have dressed well. This should be true of all Christian women. Her life is an example of the behavior suggested by Paul in his letter to Timothy. He suggests that "women adorn themselves in modest apparel, with shamefacedness and sobriety; not with broided hair, or gold, or pearls, or costly array; but (which becometh women professing godliness) with good works" (1 Timothy 2:9, 10).

5. *She was a woman of influence.*

Had not Dorcas been prominent and well-loved in the church, the disciples never would have sent for Peter to come a distance of twelve miles on foot to comfort them in their sorrow at her death. Since the miracle of her resurrection from the dead was evidently performed in order to give the gospel a better hearing in Joppa, we are inclined to believe that Dorcas was also an influential woman in the community.

6. *She typifies the new spirit of the Christian dispensation.*

In everything that is good, the New Testament goes a step further than the law of Moses. Compassion, or a feeling of pity for those who are less happy than ourselves, is a virtue which, above all, the gospel of Christ inspires and cultivates in the soul. This leads, in turn, to the performance of good works to others who are in need, and is an expression of love. The tears and gratitude of the widows, as they displayed the garments Dorcas had made for them, were a testimony to the purity of her Christian love. Dorcas' life of devotion to the needs of the poor is typical of the new spirit found in the very beginning of the New Testament church. May that spirit never die as long as the church shall stand! Christian faith always expresses itself in Christian works.

In a Nutshell

1. "Pure religion and undefiled before God and the Father is this, To visit the fatherless and widows in their affliction, and to keep himself unspotted from the world" (James 1:27).

2. Peter came to weep with those who wept, but remained to rejoice with those who rejoiced.

3. Those who receive alms are not as obliged to conceal it as are those who give alms.

4. Luke made no effort to describe the scene which followed the restoration of Dorcas to the little band of disciples she had left. If this is indescribable, what shall we say or think of that hour when all the dead in Christ shall rise to walk the golden streets of heaven?

5. Tabitha, by interpretation, had a new name. Through obedience and good works, and by the promise of God, we, too, shall have a new name (Revelation 3:12).

6. Compassion for physical suffering should pave the way for compassion for spiritual suffering.

7. Christians who use their money, time, and energy in the performance of good works are laying up for themselves "treasures in heaven, where neither moth nor rust doth corrupt, and where thieves do not break through nor steal" (Matthew 6:20).

8. We marvel that Dorcas was resurrected to a new life. Through obedience to His commands, God still resurrects to a new life those who are "dead in trespasses and sins" (Ephesians 2:1).

Discussion

1. Can a person remain a Christian long without the performance of good works?

2. What is the relationship between faith and good works?

3. What is the most important thing that ever happened to Dorcas?

Closing Prayer

Heavenly Father, as we study the life of Dorcas, we bow in humility to thank Thee for her excellent example in the performance of good works. May we, too, be led by the spirit of Christ, to minister to the needs of suffering humanity. And as we minister to the physical needs, may we be led into that larger service of relieving spiritual hunger. May we be generous in our gifts of love and service, so that Thy name may be honored throughout the world. In the name of Christ we pray. Amen.

The Leader's Notes

Chapter XI

LYDIA, A CAREER WOMAN

SCRIPTURE BACKGROUND FOR STUDY: Acts 16:1-40; Philippians 1:1—4:23

SONG SELECTIONS: 1. "Send the Light"
   2. "Tell Me the Story of Jesus"
   3. " 'Tis the Blessed Hour of Prayer" (*prayer hymn*)

PRAYER PERIOD

SCRIPTURE READING: Philippians 1

The Bible Story

The story of Lydia is short, but it is an exceedingly important study of the expansion of the early church. There are only a few verses in the book of Acts which tell us all we know about her, yet she is a prominent person in the New Testament. She is especially remembered today because of her unique place as the first Christian convert in Europe. Originally, she lived in Thyatira of Asia Minor, a city famous for its purple dyes. For business reasons, it is supposed, she had moved to Philippi in Macedonia.

We know almost nothing about Lydia's personal life, whether she was married or not; and, if so, whether or not she had children. She may have been a widow who had inherited her husband's business. We do know that she was a businesswoman, a seller of purple, and that she maintained a household. Dealing in purple, whether dye or cloth, indicates that she was a successful businesswoman and possessor of considerable wealth, for purple was expensive. It was used in the garments of royalty and the upper classes only.

Philippi was a Roman colony and one of the chief cities of Macedonia. Although cosmopolitan to some extent, the magistrates and a greater part of the inhabitants of the city were Romans. There probably was not a very large population of Jews, for no mention is made of a synagogue in the city.

The conversion of Lydia is one of the highlights of the second missionary journey of Paul. On this trip, he was accompanied by Silas and probably joined at Lystra by Timothy. There is strong indication that Luke, the writer of Acts, also traveled with Paul on this trip, for he apparently includes himself when he says "we" and "us" (Acts 16: 10-16).

When the party reached Mysia, they had every intention to continue on to Bithynia, but the Spirit of the Lord directed them elsewhere. While they lingered in Troas, "a vision appeared to Paul in the night; There stood a man of Macedonia, and prayed him, saying, Come over into Macedonia, and help us" (Acts 16:9). Not willing to be disobedient to the heavenly vision, the missionaries departed immediately for Macedonia. The first city they entered was Philippi, where they lingered until the Sabbath.

The details of the story here are scant, so we must draw upon the imagination. Why did they linger at Philippi? Did they make any contacts while awaiting the Sabbath? Where was the "man of Macedonia" who appeared in the vision? Why had the Spirit of the Lord directed them here? We cannot be sure about the answers to any of these questions, but it seems reasonable to assume that at the first port of entry into Macedonia, they lingered awaiting further direction from God. In the meantime, they probably searched the city for a synagogue or other evidences of Jewish worship. While they did not find a synagogue, they learned that a group of women met regularly for prayer on the Sabbath outside the city by the riverside. They decided to join this group.

Now, let us take a glance at the women. Who were they? Why were there no men present? Were they all proselytes of the Jewish faith? If so, how much had they learned? Why were they worshiping by the riverside and not within the city? Again, we cannot be sure of the answers. Probably Lydia herself was the leader of the group. Having learned that there was, indeed, a true and living God, not made by human hands, she may have been searching for a deeper knowledge, or she may have been teaching the other women the things she had already learned from her study of God's Word.

We do know that the group met for prayer. They needed help and direction in their search for the truth. We see the hand of God in all this. Here was a group seeking help, and here were God's messengers prepared, ready and waiting. What could be more natural than the two groups getting together? Is this not evidence of the leading of the Holy Spirit? Is it not a demonstration of God's love for His seeking children? It is clearly a fulfillment of the promise of God, made later through Paul in a letter to the church that blossomed from the tiny bud of faith, which lived in the hearts of these same women: "God shall supply all your need according to his riches in glory by Christ Jesus" (Philippians 4:19).

The record says that the missionaries "spake unto the women which resorted thither" (Acts 16:13). The immediate results are an indication of the subject matter of the sermon. They preached the whole story of Jesus—how He came as a fulfillment of the prophetic promise of a Saviour, how He had now returned to heaven, leaving behind a definite plan for the redemption of mankind. Lydia, "whose heart the Lord opened, that she attended unto the things which were spoken of Paul" (Acts 16:14), was baptized along with her household.

The next incident is an indication of the beautiful, unselfish nature of Lydia's character. She invited the missionaries to come to her home, not for a call, but to abide there for the whole duration of their stay in Philippi. Her motive was twofold. First, she longed for a greater opportunity to satisfy the hunger of her own heart for the Word of God. Second, she was anxious to be a fruit-bearing Christian—to facilitate in every way possible the spread of the gospel message to the whole area roundabout. The doors of her home were not only opened to Paul and his co-laborers, but also to all who came seeking the new religion. The missionaries were free to use her home as a teaching center for new converts.

This is almost the entire story of Lydia. One other mention is made of her hospitality to Paul and Silas. These men had been thrown into prison because they had healed a girl who was possessed with an evil spirit. After a miraculous delivery from prison and the exciting experience of converting the jailor and his household, they returned to Lydia's house for a time. There they called together the brethren, comforted them, and departed.

The church in Philippi, cradled in the home of Lydia, is one of the few churches which was not condemned, for one reason or another, by Paul when he wrote to them. On the contrary he had many commendable things to say of the Philippian Christians. He thanked God for their "fellowship in the gospel from the first day until now" (Philippians 1: 5). He spoke of them as "my brethren dearly beloved and longed for, my joy and crown" (Philippians 4:1). He commended them for their gifts of money or provisions which helped him greatly as he departed to work in other places (Philippians 4:15, 16). He commended them for their eager obedience to God's Word, saying, "Wherefore, my beloved, as ye have always obeyed, not as in my presence only, but now much more in my absence" (Philippians 2:12).

We can imagine the satisfaction Lydia had in her heart as she listened to these words from Paul. What a joy was hers in knowing that she had played such an important role in the planting of the church in Philippi! How she could thank God for sending Paul to them as they were praying down by the river!

Lydia's home was the gateway through which Christianity first entered Europe. From there it swept westward, gaining momentum and power as it traveled from country to country. Even today, we can thank God for Lydia, because it was through that open gate of her heart and home that we can trace our own opportunity to hear and obey the gospel.

Character Analysis

1. *She was a seeker after the truth.*

We do not know how Lydia, a Gentile who had lived all her life in the midst of heathenism, first learned of the true

God, but her first knowledge brought a deep longing to her heart, and she availed herself of every opportunity to learn more. She went to the place of prayer to worship God and mingle with others who believed in Him. When she first heard the matchless story of Jesus from the lips of Paul, she was not satisfied with bare details, such as could be revealed in one day, but insisted that Paul and his companions reside in her own house, so that she could hear more of the story they had to tell.

2. *She possessed many and varied capabilities.*

In an age when a woman's place was considered to be in the home, and no place else, it took courage and determination for a woman of good repute to enter the business world. Having started upon a career, it took boldness and foresight to remain in business and realize a profit. After establishing herself as a successful businesswoman, it took strength of character and will power to align herself with a minority group of worshipers. Later, the manner in which she entertained the messengers of God, strangers that they were, shows her generosity and good will toward her fellow men.

3. *She was influential in the community.*

Lydia was a wealthy woman, for she could not have carried on a purple dye business without considerable capital. Her wealth alone gave her a prominent place in the town, for in any country and in any age, whether we like it or not, money speaks. Yet we believe that, in Lydia's case, her influence sprang from her good qualities of mind and spirit, rather than from her wealth. She was the most logical person in the whole area to open the doors of her home to the missionaries, and thus contribute to the planting of the first church in Philippi. The fact that her own household unhesitatingly followed her example in obeying the gospel indicates her influence over those who were closely associated with her.

4. *She was intelligent and decisive.*

Lydia's success as a businesswoman, her withdrawal from the repulsive practices of the heathen religions, and her ready acceptance of Christianity are all testimonies to her above-normal intelligence. The ability to make good decisions quickly is also a mark of intelligence. When she heard Paul's message of salvation, she was quick to recognize it as that for which she had been searching. Her decision to become a Christian was prompt, and she lost no time in fulfilling every detail Paul pointed out as being essential to her salvation. She did not stop to consider that such a move might curtail her business or decrease her popularity with the people. She did not ask for time to think it over or to discuss it with her friends or family. Her obedience to the gospel message sprang from a heart that was sure and from a hope that was steadfast.

5. *She was hospitable.*

Immediately after her baptism, Lydia graciously invited Paul and his helpers to make her home their headquarters while they remained in the area. Paul tells us that she "constrained" them, or overcame their reluctance, as she insisted upon their acceptance of her hospitality. Notice Lydia's humility as she issued the invitation: "If ye have judged me to be faithful to the Lord, come into my house, and abide there" (Acts 16:15). Hospitality, in this sense, is distinctly a Christian virtue, and Lydia set a high example which women could safely follow today.

6. *She hungered and thirsted after righteousness.*

The life of Lydia is a perfect picture of Jesus' words, "Blessed are they which do hunger and thirst after righteousness: for they shall be filled" (Matthew 5:6). She prayed for help and God sent Paul and Silas. She hungered for more of the bread of life, and the missionaries remained in her home for extensive teaching. She thirsted for the living water, and the church was cradled in her home. She labored with Paul in the gospel, and he testified that her name was written in the book of life (Philippians 4:3). Yes, Lydia's hungering heart was satisfied. What a joy it must have been for her to hear the words of Paul in his epistle to the Philippians, "whatsoever things are true, whatsoever things are honest, whatsoever things are just, whatsoever things are pure, whatsoever things are lovely, whatsoever things are of good report; if there be any virtue, and if there be any praise, think on these things. Those things, which ye have both learned, and received, and heard, and seen in me, do: and the God of peace shall be with you" (Philippians 4:8, 9).

In a Nutshell

1. Christianity, when rightly understood and practiced, does not call us away from our business, but rather directs us in it.

2. When the heart is opened to Christ, the ear is opened to His Word, the lips are opened in prayer, the hands are opened in charity—the whole body is then ready for service.

3. Those who know something of Christ cannot help but desire to know more. Greater knowledge of Christ inspires greater service.

4. When Lydia's heart was opened to Christ, her home was opened to His messengers.

5. Money speaks—too often for the devil, but not often enough for Christ.

6. Prompt obedience to the laws of God is a mark of intelligence, maturity, and common sense.

7. Our God-given capabilities are no cause for boasting, but rather a cause for humility; they demand greater responsibility in service.

Discussion

1. Were Lydia's opportunities to be a fruit-bearing Christian greater or fewer than ours?

2. Is it easy or difficult for the modern career woman to put Christ and the church first?

3. Are we indebted in any way to Lydia?

Closing Prayer

Loving Father, we are grateful for the story of Lydia—how she opened her heart and home to Christ and His messengers. May we, the Christian women of today, be quick to recognize in her the good qualities of a fruit-bearing Christian. Help us to use our own capabilities in every way possible for the spread of the gospel of Christ. Bless our every effort in service for Thee. May we seek always to do Thy will and not our own will. We pray in Christ Jesus. Amen.

The Leader's Notes

CHAPTER XII

PRISCILLA, A SERVANT OF THE CHURCH

SCRIPTURE BACKGROUND FOR STUDY: Acts 18; Romans 16:1-5;
  1 Corinthians 16:19; 2 Timothy 4:19

SONG SELECTIONS: 1. "More About Jesus"
                        2. "Take the Name of Jesus With You"
                        3. "Sweet Hour of Prayer" (*prayer hymn*)

PRAYER PERIOD

SCRIPTURE READING: Acts 18:1-4, 24-26

The Bible Story

Priscilla is one of the most interesting women of the New Testament, considered by many to be the most prominent, for she is mentioned more often than any other woman of the early church. Her story is not told in very great detail, but it does cover a wide range of activities for Christ in three cities in three different countries—Corinth, Ephesus, and Rome. Wherever she went, she became the living embodiment of Jesus' teaching: "Let your light so shine before men, that they may see your good works, and glorify your Father which is in heaven" (Matthew 5:16).

Priscilla's husband, Aquila, was a Jew, born in Pontus. Because her name is a Roman name, most scholars think Priscilla was a Roman who married Aquila in Rome, but departed with him to Corinth when Claudius, in his cruel and unjust edict, expelled all Jews from Rome.

We do not know when these two became Christians. They might have already been Christians when Paul found them in Corinth, but the record indicates that he found them through his trade of tentmaking which was their trade also. It is possible that they were Paul's first converts in Corinth.

After preaching in Athens, where he had spoken of the unknown god, whom he said they ignorantly worshiped (Acts 17:23), Paul departed from that city and went to Corinth.

When he reached Corinth, a city of gross licentiousness, it was necessary for him to resort to his old trade of tentmaking. In this business, he met with Aquila and Priscilla, and was invited to stay in their house.

As these three sat together, day by day, weaving the goats' hair for the tents, we can picture Paul teaching Aquila and Priscilla the gospel of Jesus Christ, who came as the Messiah in fulfillment of Jewish prophecy. Every Sabbath he went to the synagogue and reasoned with both Jews and Greeks. Many of the Corinthians, including the ruler of the synagogue, believed and were baptized.

Paul remained in Corinth for about eighteen months (Acts 18:11, 18). It is believed that most of this time he lived in the home of Aquila and Priscilla. The record does not explain why, but when he left Corinth, they accompanied him. It may have been because of persecution in Corinth, for Paul and other Christians fared poorly in that city. It could have been because Paul wanted them as helpers in other places. When they came to Ephesus, Aquila and Priscilla remained and established residence while Paul continued into Galatia.

While Aquila and Priscilla lived in Ephesus, there occurred an incident which reveals, more than any other, the wisdom, tact, and devotion of these two people. Apollos, an Alexandrian Jew, who was "an eloquent man, and mighty in the scriptures" (Acts 18:24), came to Ephesus and spoke boldly in the synagogue. It appears that Apollos was well-versed in the Old Testament prophecies concerning the coming of the Messiah. Knowing John's baptism (Acts 18:25), he must have also known the subject matter of John's preaching: "Repent ye: for the kingdom of heaven is at hand" (Matthew 3:2). He believed the kingdom was soon to be approaching. What he evidently did not know was that the very thing he was preaching as being *at hand,* or in the near future, had already happened. The Messiah had already come, lived, died, arose, and ascended. The church had already been established, and His disciples were going everywhere preaching in His name.

When Aquila and Priscilla realized the limitation of

Apollos' knowledge, they determined to impart to him the full gospel story they had learned from Paul. Did the hearts of these two humble people waver in fear of offending such an eminent and brilliant evangelist? Perhaps so, but since "perfect love casteth out fear" (1 John 4:18), they "took him unto them, and expounded unto him the way of God more perfectly" (Acts 18:26).

What was the result? Apollos accepted their teaching and became one of the gospel's most able exponents. When he left Ephesus, the brethren wrote letters asking the disciples to receive him. Wherever he went, he "helped them much which had believed through grace: for he mightily convinced the Jews, and that publickly, shewing by the scriptures that Jesus was Christ" (Acts 18:27, 28). Paul wrote of him to the Corinthians, "I have planted, Apollos watered; but God gave the increase" (1 Corinthians 3:6). Had not Priscilla and her husband been bold in approaching this eloquent man of God and true in their teaching, he might have spent his entire lifetime preaching only part of the truth. With their help, he became the most outstanding evangelist of the early church, winning many converts to Christ, both Jews and Greeks.

On Paul's third missionary journey, he stopped at Ephesus and found a church flourishing in the home of Aquila and Priscilla. As he journeyed through Asia, he came to Philippi where he wrote his first letter to the Corinthian church in which he sent greetings from the churches in Asia, and from Aquila and Priscilla "with the church that is in their house" (1 Corinthians 16:19).

For reasons unknown to us, this faithful Christian couple sometime later moved to Rome, where their home again became the meeting place for the disciples. In the Roman letter, written by Paul from Corinth, and sent by Phebe, he says, "Greet Priscilla and Aquila my helpers in Christ Jesus: who have for my life laid down their own necks: unto whom not only I give thanks, but also all the churches of the Gentiles. Likewise greet the church that is in their house" (Romans 16:3-5).

The last we hear of Aquila and Priscilla, they have left

Rome and returned to Ephesus. When Paul was a prisoner in Rome, he wrote his second letter to Timothy, who was evidently in Ephesus (2 Timothy 1:18), in which he said, "Salute Prisca and Aquila" (2 Timothy 4:19).

Through the years, Paul had a close fellowship with these two. The number of times he mentioned their names in his letters, the greetings he sent to them, and the commendable things he said of their work all indicate the warm feeling of friendship he felt for them. In writing Priscilla's name the last time from Rome, he used the diminutive form "Prisca," thus indicating his closeness to them. The fact that they "laid down their own necks" (Romans 16:4) for Paul shows their esteem for him.

In summarizing the story of Priscilla, we must conclude that her prominence was due not only to her religious and scholarly endowments, but also to her sacrificial nature. She lived in a time when Christians faced persecution on every hand, but she was not afraid. In two cities in which she lived, the Christians used her home for their meeting place. Even though she was kept busy with her home duties and with tentmaking, she still found time to open the doors of her home to the church and to messengers of the church. Many are the honors which have been heaped upon Priscilla by early Christian writers. They broke all conventionalities by three times placing her name before that of her husband. This indicates that she was held in exceedingly high esteem.

Character Analysis

1. *She was industrious.*

One of the first things we learn of Priscilla is that she and her husband were tentmakers. With the usual cares of her home, her trade, and her many works for the Lord, we can see that she was a busy woman. There is virtue and happiness in honest work. The inclination to work by his side made her a joy to her husband. The inclination to work in the kingdom of God made her a joy to Paul and many other preachers and evangelists in the early church.

2. *She was hospitable.*

Had not Priscilla exercised a beautiful spirit of hospitality, she might never have known the gospel of Christ. Having met Paul in the course of business, she was gracious in her invitation that he abide in their home. In so doing, she brought a blessing to her own home and opened the doors of opportunity to countless others in Corinth. "Be not forgetful to entertain strangers: for thereby some have entertained angels unawares" (Hebrews 13:2). It is likely that many other travelers for Christ, including Apollos, found a welcome in the home of Aquila and Priscilla.

3. *She was studious.*

Priscilla had a mind that was open for learning. Having married a Jew, she became acquainted with the Jewish religion, was perhaps a proselyte. We do not know when she became a Christian, but whenever it was, she applied herself diligently to learning all she could about this wonderful new way of life. She must have drunk thirstily of the fountain of Paul's wisdom as she worked day by day with him in the tent-making trade, and listened to him reasoning with the Jews and Greeks in the synagogue.

4. *She was zealous for Christ.*

Once Priscilla knew the gospel of Christ, she devoted her whole life to the spread of its message. Wherever she went, her home and heart were open to the church. When she first heard the eloquent preaching of Apollos in the synagogue at Ephesus, her zeal for the truth that is in Christ impelled her to approach him for the purpose of instruction in the way of Christ. She was ready to lay down her life for the sake of the gospel if it became necessary.

5. *She was apt to teach.*

Being "apt to teach" is one of the qualifications which Paul listed as necessary for one who desires the office of an elder (1 Timothy 3:2), but this quality is not limited to the eldership. Many women of the early church were teachers, Priscilla not the least among them. She studied the Word of

God in humility, but proclaimed it boldly. She was earnest but tactful in "expounding" the way of God to Apollos. Her teaching was fortified by her own life of service and love to the church and the messengers of God.

6. *She was a servant of the church.*

Paul speaks of Aquila and Priscilla as his "helpers in Christ Jesus . . . unto whom not only I give thanks, but also all the churches of the Gentiles" (Romans 16:3, 4). This is an intimation that many of the Gentile churches had received numerous services from these two Christian workers. The fact that the church met in their home gave them ample opportunity to serve in many capacities—opportunities they would not let pass.

7. *She was faithful.*

Priscilla and her husband were faithful Christians through many years. These were trying years, for it was the age of persecution, and Christians were unpopular wherever they went. Their first move from Rome to Corinth was because of the persecution of the Jews. Likely all the other moves were because of the persecution of Christians. We do not know the time or manner of their death. It is possible that persecution finally caught up with them and they died by the sword, as did countless thousands of the early Christians. In this event they could have said along with Paul, "For to me to live is Christ, and to die is gain" (Philippians 1:21).

In a Nutshell

1. The trade of Priscilla and Aquila was tentmaking, but their business was Christ.

2. Zeal for Christ without knowledge is of no effect (Romans 10:2). The opposite is also true.

3. Persecution for one's belief does not prove that he is right.

4. "Blessed are they which are persecuted for righteousness' sake: for theirs is the kingdom of heaven" (Matthew 5:10).

5. An idle mind is the devil's workshop.

6. "Study to shew thyself approved unto God, a workman that needeth not to be ashamed, rightly dividing the word of truth" (2 Timothy 2:15).

7. One teaches more by what he does than by what he says.

8. How *long* one lives is not important, only *how* he lives.

Discussion

1. Why does the Bible leave out so much of the life stories of so many interesting people?

2. Is every Christian obligated to teach?

3. How many people does it take to make a church?

Closing Prayer

Our Father, we praise Thy name for all Thy mercy and goodness to us. We are thankful for the church with her message of salvation, and for Christ and His love for us. We are thankful for the steadfastness of the early Christians as they faced persecution and death for the sake of their belief. May they be an inspiration to us when temptation comes to us in small ways. Help us to be willing and ready to suffer for the sake of Christ when it is necessary. May we use Priscilla as an example in service, hospitality, and love for the church in our work today, for it is in the name of Christ we pray. Amen.

The Leader's Notes